What a powerfully written b I needed! Sharon brings the tr able, encouraging, and challenging way. It is a must read for anyone feeling stuck in the face of life's challenges (and aren't we all at times?)! *Arise and Climb the Mountain* will encourage you to bravely persevere through whatever difficulty you are facing, continue to move forward, and see what God has in store for you. Sharon has beautifully weaved together her own personal stories and powerful biblical truths into a wonderful guide for anyone wanting to deepen their faith journey while persevering through the hardships of life.

—Carolyn Munson

Arise and Climb the Mountain is an amazing book! I have been struggling with my faith for the past two and a half years due to the loss of my son. Scripture has been quoted perfectly in conjunction with the author's experiences. It was food for my spirit. It was an easy read with powerful words. I wanted more and I am looking forward to her next book.

—Mirtica Aldave

Sharon thoughtfully brings us on a spiritual adventure through the picturesque Adirondacks as she guides us through her own faith journey of pain and joy. It is a refreshing workout for the mind and soul!

—Jill Lind

The book is so readable and profound yet straightforward so that even a new believer will gain a clear understanding of God's love, forgiveness, and plan for our lives.

—Donna O'Connor

The book gave me a visual picture of God's outpouring love during times of deep pain and disappointment. It made me visualize myself (the imperfect me) and God's deep love for me. It gave me a picture of God never letting me go, tightly holding my hand, walking beside me, and never ever leaving me behind. It was a great reminder of God's deep and unchanging love for me, I do not need to fear ever being torn away from Him.

—Teresa Pliszka

The book is very meaty for the believer and yet approachable for the non-believer. Sharon's steady spiritual insights that kept me invested in the book.

—Ryan Schneider

The book is an easy read, yet full of depth, heart, and transparency. It is powerfully vulnerable and full of hope. Sharon's openness fosters our openness, and her reflections inspire us to reflect, not deflect. When we are honest with ourselves and God about where we are at, we can then get past the boulders and move forward where he wants us to be. Sharon's example is inspiring and motivating and reflects God through and through.

—Jeannette Brennan

What a magnificent story! One minute I am reading the Bible and the next I am reading a love story, the next a manual for survival, the next a devotional, and then a comedy. Thank you, Sharon, for writing this book and sharing it with all of us. It is such a beautiful blessing, and I can't wait to read it again. I will bring my box of tissues for tears of sadness and joy.

—Debi Anderson

When I read the book, tears flowed and I had goosebumps. It was an affirmation to me how deeply God loves me and has used everything in my life to draw me to Himself. It showed me how God teaches me about His character and faithfulness so I can share my testimony about his work in and through me.

—Lisa Wetjen

This book shows us how we can bring our burdens (mountains) to the Lord and let Him take care of them. It is a matter of faith and trust. This is a masterpiece that everyone should read.

—Rosie Cascundo

Arise and Climb the Mountain is a spiritually uplifting, must-read book. Reading the book and completing the study guide brought me to a deeper level of faith. It helped me recognize that at the times when I thought I was alone God was always there to keep me on the right path in my journey with Him!

—Sue Sexton

Carpets of pine needles, sparkling rocks, sun-splashed ridges, and clean mountain scents prompted me to sneak my feet into Sharon's hiking boots during her mountain climb. I was drawn to the challenge, and I wanted to hike up with her to see what the outcome would be. As Sharon stripped off layers and revealed raw edges, I realized that her tough constitution and God-fueled will made her focus on Him rather than on her troubles She demonstrated many examples of God's deliverance: kept promises, answered prayers, and healing. I wanted the same for myself and through her book, I grew in faith. Her shared testimonies instilled hope and drew out my own accountability. I hungered for a deeper relationship with God. Sharon's book will speak to every Christian reader in a personal perspective. You will be encouraged to rely on God during your own life-challenges. Sharon's pages directed me back to God when I drifted toward my disappointments. I finished this book feeling refreshed and recharged.

—Holly Scudder

Sharon has a way of gently guiding a person in any season of life to God's Word for encouragement, hope, guidance, and truth to cope with the stumbling blocks they come across as disciples for Christ. I could almost feel her gentle hand on my shoulder nudging me toward God's truth in His Word. I wholeheartedly testify that despite what life places in her path, Sharon seeks the Lord's counsel and then listens, waits, prays, and goes where God is guiding her with a bold, courageous faith. This book is a conduit of inspiration to anyone who reads it to keep pressing on, even if one cannot see the forest for the trees.

—Lisa Lickwar

ARISE,
AND CLIMB
THE
MOUNTAIN

ARISE,
AND CLIMB
THE
MOUNTAIN

When God doesn't move the mountains,
He gives you faith to climb them

SHARON ELEANOR TODD

Published by Redemption Press, PO Box 427, Enumclaw, WA 98022.
Toll-Free (844) 2REDEEM (273-3336)

Redemption Press is honored to present this title in partnership with the author. The views expressed or implied in this work are those of the author. Redemption Press provides our imprint seal representing design excellence, creative content, and high-quality production.

The author has tried to recreate events, locales, and conversations from memories of them. In order to maintain their anonymity, in some instances the names of individuals, some identifying characteristics, and some details may have been changed, such as physical properties, occupations, and places of residence.

Cover photo provided by photographer Jonathan Esper at www.wildernessphotographs.com

ISBN 13: 978-1-64645-198-2 (Paperback)

Library of Congress Catalog Card Number: 2022908521

CONTENTS

DEDICATION & ACKNOWLEDGMENTS

Jesus looked at them and said, "With man this is impossible, but with God all things are possible."
Matthew 19:26 NIV

This book is dedicated to my extraordinary parents,
Gordon Carl Todd and Eleanor Holden Todd.

They have instilled in our family a deep abiding love for Christ, a passion for the Adirondack Mountains, and a tenacious mindset to persevere through life's challenges.

Special acknowledgment to my faithful friends who covered the writing of this book in prayer, gave valuable feedback, and encouraged me all along the journey. I thank God for the gift of your friendship.

PREFACE

"Forever Wild"
The Adirondack Mountains of Northern New York

"The mountains are calling, and I must go," is a quote from John Muir that resonates in the depths of my soul. This book will reveal my passion for the Adirondack Mountains, a special place of healing and restoration, as well as provide a feast for the senses. The Adirondacks are widely known for sweet clean air, crystal clear lakes, and majestic mountains everywhere you look. My family has lived, worked, and vacationed in the Adirondacks for generations. We are drawn to the mountains and lakes because they are such an integral part of our DNA. Just being in the Adirondacks makes us feel refreshed and closer to our Lord. The pristine beauty of the Adirondack Park is filled with over 3,000 lakes and more than thirty-thousand miles of brooks, streams, and rivers. It has six million acres of land, lakes, mountains, forest, wetland, and streams. The Adirondack Park is the largest protected park in the lower forty-eight states.

Presidents, pastors, photographers, painters, and poets have long been inspired by the beauty of the Adirondacks. As an artist, I often experience moments of inspiration as I hike in the mountains or sit on the dock early in the morning. Ralph Waldo Emerson wrote a poem in 1858 about Follensby Pond after he camped there with several friends who were artists, writers, and philosophers. The location is just a short drive from our camp, and it is easy to see why Emerson became enamored with the area. The Adirondacks have a long history of being a place of adventure and healing for visitors and residents alike.

Rev. William H. H. Murray was a pastor who wrote the book *Adventures in the Wilderness* in 1869, which described his experience of drawing closer to God in the Adirondacks. Murray found it was restorative to escape busy city life and renew in the fresh mountain air. His book resonated with stressed-out and overworked urban dwellers, and thousands visited the Adirondack Mountains in a desperate search of renewal.

Many presidents and politicians have also frequented the Adirondacks for a time of rest and recreation. President Calvin Coolidge's 1926 summer White House was at the White Pine Camp, one of the Great Camps on a secluded lake in the Adirondacks down the road from Lake Titus.

After hiking Mount Marcy, the highest mountain among the famous forty-six High Peaks of the Adirondack Mountains, I understood why adventurous hikers come from all around the world to climb this majestic mountain. It demands physical perseverance, but the view from the summit makes the trek entirely worth it. On September 12, 1901, Vice President Theodore Roosevelt was climbing Mount Marcy with his family and an Adirondack guide when he received a telegram that President McKinley was gravely ill. It was imperative for Roosevelt to return to Washington, DC, to become the next president.

Another aspect to enjoy in the Adirondack region is the great history of the Winter Olympics. The Winter Olympics were first hosted in Lake Placid in 1932, and then returned in 1980 to showcase an unforgettable win by Team USA over the world champion Soviet Union ice hockey team. The young USA team, with mostly college students, had only practiced together for six months. You can imagine everyone's surprise when they won (4–3) in the last second of the game. This legendary Olympic ice hockey upset is remembered by most Americans as an extraordinary victory for America. Our family fondly recalls that incredible win when the USA underdog team climbed their metaphorical mountain of uncertainty and became victorious heroes. By the grace of God and countless hours of rigorous training, they truly accomplished the impossible!

In this book, I will bring you on an adventure through the Adirondacks. However, one must experience the mountains to understand why it is an ideal haven for physical, spiritual, and emotional healing. After reading my book, I hope you will visit the Adirondack Mountains and climb one of the forty-six High Peaks so you can personally experience refreshment and renewal in this remarkable place.

Climb One of the Forty-Six High Peaks
Adirondack Mountains

Marcy 5344 - Algonquin 5114 - Haystack 4960 - Skylight 4926 - Whiteface 4867 - Dix 4857 - Gray 4840 - Iroquois Peak 4840 - Basin 4827 - Gothics 4736 - Colden 4714 - Giant 4627 - Nippletop 4620 - Santanoni 4607 - Redfield 4606 - Wright Peak 4580 - Saddleback 4515 - Panther 4442 - Table Top 4427 - Rocky Peak 4420 - Macomb 4405 - Armstrong 4400 - Hough 4400 - Seward 4361 - Marshall 4360 - Allen 4340 - Big Slide 4240 - Esther 4240 - Upper Wolf Jaw 4185 - Lower Wolf Jaw 4175 - Street 4166 - Phelps 4161 - Donaldson 4140 - Seymour 4120 - Sawteeth 4100 - Cascade 4098 - South Dix 4060 - Porter 4059 - Colvin 4057 - Emmons 4040 - Dial 4020 - Grace Peak 4012 - Blake Peak 3960 - Cliff 3960 - Nye 3895 - Couchsachraga 3820

www.adkforty-sixer.org

Thousands of tired, nerve-shaken, over-civilized people are beginning to find out going to the mountains is "going home," that wilderness is a necessity. . .
—John Muir

INTRODUCTION

These trials will show that your faith is genuine. It is being tested as fire tests and purifies gold—though your faith is far more precious than mere gold. So when your faith remains strong through many trials, it will bring you much praise and glory and honor on the day when Jesus Christ is revealed to the whole world.

1 Peter 1:7 NLT

During the writing this book, our world was turned upside down with the COVID pandemic, job loss, supply chain problems, and widespread economic distress. Within the blink of an eye, our lives as we knew them were forever altered and the "new normal" was anything but normal. Navigating a long season of unwelcomed change was all too familiar to me. In the past, I endured a season of social isolation, loss of identity, grief, divorce, social media lies, unemployment, and fear over the uncertainty of the future. There have been blessings and challenges around giving up my career and independence to care for elderly parents and family. I know the profound loss of having my well-organized world radically altered and turned upside down. But God can use our worst experiences and turn them around for good. In fact, many of my disappointments were redeemed through writing this book to encourage others who are struggling to hold on to hope.

The inspiration for this book began on a personal retreat, which turned into a hiking adventure in the Adirondack Mountains. It should have been a quick and effortless hike that day, but an unexpected injury to my foot changed my pace. I believe God slowed me down so He could have my full attention. While I slowly hiked the trail to Elephant's Head Mountain, my mind was flooded with countless memories of God's faithfulness over the years. I was overwhelmed with gratitude despite the pain of my foot injury. What started as an easy hike that autumn day turned into a faith-filled trek of perseverance toward the summit.

Arise, and Climb the Mountain is a series of non-sequential inspirational stories. This book invites you on a personal journey recalling God's faithfulness in the past, identifying present struggles, and applying life lessons for a better future. The beginning of each chapter features just a portion of my Adirondack hiking adventure broken down into different scenes. Each scene contains powerful gospel truths and Adirondack metaphors that are discussed further in the adjoining chapter. My desire is for every person to embrace the fullness of what God has for them and not be content with mediocrity.

This world may be constantly changing, but the good news of Jesus Christ remains unwavering and true. As Christ followers, we can fix our eyes higher than our circumstances, and God will instruct us how to actively grow in our faith. The questions we can ask God during any crisis are, *What are you teaching me, What are you showing me,* and *How do you want me to grow through this trial?* Instead of pleading with God to remove the hardship, we can pray, asking God to strengthen our ability to persevere.

The "Transformational Trek" study guide contains journaling questions to help you continue your spiritual quest and can be downloaded from my website at www.SharonEleanorTodd.com. I recommend that you read the book first, and then work through the entirety of the study guide. You will not be required to flip back and forth from the book chapters to the guide questions. The study guide materials will flow together better as a separate unit. I'm praying you will experience the presence of the Lord as the mountain streams of His living water refresh your weary souls. Jesus will lead you through the Adirondack wilderness and turn your sorrow into joy, defeat into victory, and despair into hope. As you surrender every painful memory and choose to follow Christ, He will begin healing your hearts on the inside as He transforms your fear into faith. Be encouraged, for we are more than conquerors in Christ Jesus, and we *will* be overcomers!

My journey of faith has been analogous to a strenuous hike through peaks and valleys in my beloved Adirondack Mountains. I started my trips there as a child and have continued this family tradition almost every year throughout my life. Since the stories in my book are not in chronological order, this timeline will provide an overview of my major life events for greater clarity. I grew up in Connecticut and attended college in Michigan, where I met and married my husband. We moved to Chicago to pursue our careers and dreams, and, sadly, divorced after many years. It was during that transitional period in my life when the Lord planted a new dream in my heart to go into full-time ministry and eventually write a book to help Christians struggling with grief and loss. Using God's Word to strengthen people's faith muscles and restore their hope during difficult seasons and life transitions fueled my passion for discipleship care. I enjoyed a fulfilling and fruitful ministry for almost a decade, until the Spirit gave me a new calling. Little did I realize He would lead me back to Connecticut to care for my family and elderly parents, a mission of love for the last 13 years and counting. What started out as an overwhelming assignment eventually transitioned into an extraordinary blessing. In the quiet, early morning hours, before my caregiver duties started for the day, I was able to write this book. The Lord delights in using our life transitions for gospel transformations. God's ways are higher than our ways, and His timing is always perfect. Reflecting over my life story, I can see how the Holy Spirit tenderly gathered all the broken pieces of my shattered dreams and created a beautiful mosaic for His glory.

CLIMB THE MOUNTAIN
SCENE 1

The cheerful sound of birds singing outside my window woke me up right before the sun lifted its radiant head over the mountain. The old wooden stairs creaked as I slowly descended to the main floor to see the sunrise. I made it to the dock with my steaming-hot cup of coffee and slid into the Adirondack chair facing the eastern mountains. It is the perfect front-row seat to view the sunrise with great anticipation. The rising sun casts sparkles of light like diamonds on the water. I love my mornings on the dock at Lake Titus, nestled inside the northern tip of the Adirondack Mountains. It is one of my favorite places to meet with God and rest in His presence.

Every morning at Lake Titus is a beautiful display of God's artistry in creation. However, this morning seemed extra special for some reason. It began with a beaver gliding by the dock in the stillness of the morning. "Be still and know that I am God," from Psalm 46:10, echoed in my mind as I gazed upon the peaceful scene. The surrounding forest was bursting with vibrant fall colors. Red, yellow, orange, and green leaves reflected in the still water as the brilliant sun peeked over the mountain. It was breathtaking. The lake was smooth like glass before me, a vivid picture of how to be still before the Lord. I whispered, "Good morning, Lord. I'm here to soak in the goodness of your presence."

As if on cue, a gentle breeze flowed down from the mountains and skillfully moved through the copper chimes, causing them to play a syncopated, beautiful, low bass melody. It was as if the Holy Spirit whispered back to me in music, *Beloved, I love you, too, and my presence is here with you.*

As the sun rose higher, the waters awakened with gentle waves from the wind. Lily pads danced with their different hues of green, purple, and yellow with white flowers, moving in tandem with the sailboat mooring ball, its head bobbing against the waves. The "forever wild" Adirondack Mountains were adorned with a lovely covering of pine, maple, and birch trees as far as the eye could see. Crickets chirped enthusiastically, birds sang melodic songs, and the Adirondack air smelled cedar-tree sweet. My lungs felt cleansed as I inhaled the fresh mountain air.

Sipping my coffee, I listened to the sounds of nature. A loon cried out in the distance; it was a forlorn-sounding call as if to say to its beloved, *Where are you?* Loons are believed to have one mate in their lifetime, and while sometimes they swim on different sides of the lake, they call out day and night through various calls. This morning, I listened to the loon call, *Where are you?* and then I saw the happy couple swim toward each other out in front of my dock. It was sweet to watch them circle around while they dunked their heads down in the water, looking for fish. Loons cry out only when they cannot see each other. Once they see their spouse, they are silently content, knowing their presence is near. Loons are especially vocal at night when it is dark outside. They communicate because they want the closeness of their beloved for comfort and safety and to feel loved in the darkness of the night.

It was a fleeting thought, but I couldn't help but wonder if my radical leap of faith to uproot everything and leave Chicago would have been easier if I'd had a supportive husband by my side. At this very moment, I felt so alone. I know my thinking was foolish as I had never felt emotionally supported or loved in my marriage. The absence of sharing a mutual love for Christ was an immense disappointment in our relationship. Ironically, I felt a more profound sense of loneliness in my marriage than I have ever felt as a single woman. Later in life, I realized that healthy relationships cannot be one-sided. A Christ-centered marriage requires a commitment of three—husband, wife, and the Holy Spirit—to create the kind of lasting intimacy we all crave. Instantly, the Lord reassured me that I am never alone, for He is always with me.

Since my divorce, I have found contentment in my singleness and great peace and security in His presence. It is a comfort to know I can cry out to Jesus during the dark nights of the soul, and He draws near. He promises to never leave us or forsake us, so even when we don't see or feel His love, we can know by faith that He is right by our side. God listens intently to every prayer, wrapping His loving arms around us and protecting our hearts from feeling alone. There is no love more satisfying than Christ's love. As I sat worshiping and pouring out my heart to God, I heard in my spirit again, *Be still and know that I am God.*

God knew this was exactly what I needed. Earlier that morning I was feeling bone-tired and utterly depleted. I just needed Jesus. When I opened the Bible to the gospel of Luke, every word was living water to my parched soul. The Word refreshed me as I sat reflecting on Christ's ministry of love and compassion to the brokenhearted. My heart was awakened afresh with a holy fire. As I embraced the goodness of His healing presence, I felt lighter, stronger, and thankful for my time away from all of life's demands. It felt good to exhale all the stress I had been bottling up inside me, then inhale the goodness of God through His living Word. The rhythmic breathing of *stress out* and *Jesus in* was like waves of healing water as I released the toxic memories.

Just then, my eyes glided over the mountain range surrounding the lake and focused on Elephant's Head, a small mountain on the south end of our lake. I felt a gentle nudge inside to go climb it. I pondered what to do; I could either continue to sit here in the residue of sorrow, or I could embark on a hiking adventure. The decision was clear. Without hesitation, I bolted up from my Adirondack chair and swiftly headed inside to pack a small backpack with a water bottle and travel hat. As I headed toward my yellow kayak near the boathouse, I looked up into the sky and shouted, "The adventure begins!" I was smiling ear to ear. Then I picked up my paddle and eased into the kayak, declaring with eager anticipation, "Let's go!"

CHAPTER 1

HEALING WATERS
OF GOD'S LOVE

*My child, pay attention to what I say. Listen carefully to
my words. Don't lose sight of them. Let them penetrate deep
into your heart, for they bring life to those who find them,
and healing to their whole body. Guard your heart above
all else, for it determines the course of your life.*

Proverbs 4:20–23 NLT

Reviving Dry Bones

Despite how we feel, the truth is that God does everything out
of a heart of love for us. I have often reminded myself of this
powerful quote by Anne Graham Lotz: "The times when you and
I can't trace His hand of purpose, we must trust His heart of love!"[1]

Believing this hard truth was put to the test in my life. Right after
a mountaintop ministry experience, the real Enemy set my world on
fire to see if my faith would hold up when the forest surrounding me
burned to the ground. I was wounded, exhausted, and confused as
my world radically changed in an unexpected way. After the flames
died down, it felt surreal as everything that was familiar was gone and
so much of what was cherished was lost. Just like the aftermath of a
raging forest fire, the skeletons of the trees in the forest looked like a
valley of dry bones. What was once lush, vibrant, and teeming with
life was now an ash-filled wasteland.

Without a shadow of doubt, the Lord called me to trust Him in greater ways than I had ever trusted Him when I left Chicago. I took a deep breath and stepped out in raw faith. It was a bold and scary decision, but God was with me. He never left me for a second. God, in His infinite faithfulness, guided and provided for me. One day, when I walked out to the lighthouse on Foster Beach and looked back at the Chicago skyline, I knew it was time to pack up my belongings and leave. I felt weary and burned to a crisp. When all my strength was gone, my heavenly Father's everlasting arms brought me home to the Adirondack wilderness for a season of rest.

Our remote family camp at Lake Titus was the perfect place for me to experience refreshment and renewal. I spent a long time reading Scripture on the dock, soaking in God's promises, which began to restore my charred and wounded identity with His healing balm of truth. I looked around and gazed upon the beauty of the mountains, reflecting on the still waters. He refreshed me with these words: "Pay attention to what I say; turn your ear to my words. Do not let them out of your sight, keep them within your heart; for they are life to those who find them and health to one's whole body" (Proverbs 4:20–22). I desperately needed the Holy Spirit to comfort me with His gentle reassurance in the Scriptures.

Just then, a biblical story from 1 Kings 17–19 came to mind about how the prophet Elijah also suffered from exhaustion and discouragement after he experienced several ministry victories. First God answered Elijah's prayer to end the drought, then defeated the prophets of Baal. Both events were glorious victories for the kingdom of God, but they also took an emotional, spiritual, and physical toll on Elijah. He was so depleted that he despaired when he learned Jezebel was planning to kill him, so he fled into the wilderness. I am sure he felt like dry bones when he crashed hard and cried out, "I have had enough, Lord," and then fell asleep. God, in His great mercy, had an angel of the Lord give him food and rest. After a time of rest and refreshment, the Lord spoke to Elijah in a "gentle whisper" (1 Kings 19:12).

This story reminds us that God is with us on our mountaintop victories as well as our low points in the wilderness. God knows that we, in our humanity, will grow weary and need to retreat from time to time. I completely identified with Elijah's emotional and physical exhaustion. Toward the end of my time in Chicago, I remember a particularly difficult day. As I sat in my parked car in front of my apartment building, everything I had been bottling up inside for a long time finally overwhelmed me. It was like the pressure tank was beyond overloaded, and I burst out with heavy, uncontrollable sobs. I slammed my hand against the steering wheel and screamed at the top of my lungs, "God, I can't do this anymore! I followed you in loving obedience, so why are you allowing this to happen? Where are you, and why aren't you coming to my defense?"

Have you ever felt spiritually or emotionally dry and wondered, *Where is God?* Let me assure you, my friend, He is right there with you in the valley of dry bones. I try to imagine God actively holding my heart in His loving hands so I will not become hardened from suffering. Even when you feel as though your prayers are falling on deaf ears, you can cling to this truth with confidence and assurance: Christ is in you, beside you, in front of you, and behind you as your rear guard. He is walking with you through this desolate valley, and He will guide you to greener pastures. You are His precious child, and He will not abandon you.

Israel also experienced spiritual dry bones when the Jews were in Babylonian captivity. They had lost all hope. Their dire circumstances overwhelmed them, and they lost sight of the truth of God's faithfulness, unfailing love, and sovereign plan. They allowed their horrible circumstances to erode their trust in His covenant promise.

We can easily do the same when we are emotionally depleted and spread too thin. The prophet Ezekiel spoke the Word of God to Israel, and the Holy Spirit breathed life back into their dry bones. Ezekiel 37:4–6 says, "Dry bones, listen to the word of the Lord! This is what the Sovereign Lord says: 'Look! I am going to put breath into you and make you live again! Then you will know that I am the Lord.'" No matter how emotionally numb or dry you may feel inside, the Lord can revive you.

All of us have our own mountains to climb, and sometimes the challenges we face seem insurmountable. Rest assured, if you trust and believe in God's promises in His Word, you can climb any personal mountains in your life through the power of the Holy Spirit. But how do you do that, especially if you're emotionally depleted and spiritually spent? It requires a renewed relationship with Jesus so He can replace your fear with faith.

So how is your relationship with Christ right now? Have you made a decision to follow Him? Are you madly in love with Jesus or just lukewarm about Him? Do you feel spiritually dry? Are you struggling with a sin issue that is hindering your spiritual walk? Do you need help radically prioritizing your life to what truly matters from God's perspective? Have you walked away from God completely? Honestly, your starting point doesn't matter. God can bring about a profound awakening as you embark on a spiritual renewal journey with Him. You just need to take the first step of faith.

Personal renewal begins with returning to your first love—getting back to the place of relationship with Christ that is full of hope, joy, victory, and freedom. Is this what you desire? Are you brave enough to pray a dangerous prayer for spiritual revival? It may not be for the faint of heart, but I guarantee it will be worth it.

When you seek the Lord, He will answer your prayers with the adventure of a lifetime. "'For I know the plans I have for you,' declares the Lord, 'plans to prosper you and not to harm you, plans to give you hope and a future. Then you will call on me and come and pray to me, and I will listen to you. You will seek me and find me when you seek me with all your heart'" (Jeremiah 29:11–13 NIV). His adventure may take you deeper into the wilderness, but He promises to guide you. Often it is in our wilderness experiences, like Elijah, when we can hear the gentle whispers of God's still small voice. What a powerful promise! The Lord is never too busy to hear your prayers, and He is eagerly listening to every word. If you seek God with your whole heart, you *will* find Him with His loving arms open wide.

Will you pray with me?

Lord, you are sovereign over all things in heaven and on earth. I praise your holy name for all that you have done in the past and all that you will do in the future. My life is in your hands. Please help me to trust you unconditionally, serve you sacrificially, and follow you with obedience. I want to decrease so your glory will increase. Would you allow me to be your ambassador so I can shine the light of Christ to those around me? I want our relationship to be unhindered by my sin. Shine your light on the deep-rooted idols of my heart so I can turn away from them. I love you, Lord, and I am willing to surrender whatever you ask of me. May my testimony be a witness to your mercy and grace so I can encourage and bless others along the journey. To you be the glory, Lord, now and forevermore.

Returning to Your First Love

Our idols desire to consume our thoughts, emotionally drain us, and distract us from God's bigger plan. At their root, idols of the heart are commonly entrenched in fear or pride. Bill Bright said, "Whatever preoccupies your thoughts and your schedule is quite likely your 'god.'"[2] The warning God gave the believers in Ephesus about idols long ago is still true for us today. Modern-day idols carry significant spiritual consequences, and that is why we need to take a closer look at the warning given in the book of Revelation.

Revelation 2:1–7 is a warning written to the church in Ephesus to move away from the idols of their hearts and return to their first love. Ephesus was a large, cosmopolitan city with volumes of international commerce and arts. It was one of the most influential cities in the Roman Empire, probably comparable to a city the size of Chicago today. The Ephesian believers were leading busy lives, "doing ministry" in the community, but many of the believers had lost their singlular devotion to and love for God. Revelation 2:3–5 (NLT) says, "You have patiently suffered for me without quitting. But I have this complaint against you. You don't love me or each other as you did at first! Look how far you have fallen! Turn back to me and work as you did at first." The believers' love for God and each other was wearing thin. The people in the church at Ephesus were serving with the wrong focus because they had fallen away from their first love—Christ.

When my Chicago church tour group followed in the footsteps of the Apostle Paul, we visited the ruins of Ephesus. After Pastor Ron May led a devotion on Revelation 2 about turning away from our first love, we had time to reflect and journal. I vividly remember experiencing conviction from the Holy Spirit that, while I passionately loved the Lord and had dedicated my life to furthering the kingdom of God, my heart was becoming divided between pleasing God and pleasing man. At that time, I realized I had shifted my focus from trying to please my ex-husband to trying to please others as I worked long hours in church ministry. The idol of people-pleasing is a constant treadmill, which led me to an ugly place of frustration, exhaustion, and disappointment.

Serving in ministry is one of the greatest blessings, but without proper boundaries it can be all-consuming. People's needs will always far outnumber the hours in any given day. I sincerely wanted to please the pastoral leaders and the people in the church. It felt impossible to manage a healthy work-life balance. Amid the tension between pleasing God and man, compassion, fatigue, and physical exhaustion started to settle deep into my bones. My heart was still on fire for Jesus, but I was a weary soldier who had weathered many ministry battles and victories. In hindsight, it was out of God's great mercy and love for me that He gave me the clarity to resign from my job and take a season of much needed rest.

Have you ever served God, the church, or someone else with the wrong heart motivation? Perhaps you started out with the right focus but capitulated to people's expectations and pressure. Have you ever served because you desired people's recognition, praise, or approval? If you are honest, you will answer yes because we have all fallen short in the area of man-pleasing. We are all fallen creatures in need of God's grace every single day of our lives. God is jealous for our affection, and He desires our undivided devotion. He knows when our focus on Him has been displaced by other priorities and desires. More than anything or anyone else in the world, He wants us to return to our first love and adore Him.

We all have heart-longings for something greater, whether it is a relationship, a promise, or a dream. "Hope deferred makes a heart sick, but a dream fulfilled is a tree of life" (Proverbs 13:12 NLT). When our dreams go unfulfilled, our heart begins to feel sick. In Hebrew, the word for sick also means "severely wounded or grieved," depending on the context. If we are constantly preoccupied with pleasing people, this can be a fast track toward intense disappointment. Whatever we desire more than a relationship with Christ has taken a wrongful place of worship. The object of our affection can grow into a modern-day idol in our heart as we unknowingly place God's love on the back burner.

It doesn't matter how long we have had a relationship with Christ, the number of spiritual victories we've had, or in what capacity we are serving the church. When our focus shifts away from God's priorities and His love, it is guaranteed that the wellspring of God's love in our heart will run dry. It doesn't matter what our marital status is—married, widowed, divorced, or single—God still wants us to love Him completely with total devotion. He wants to be our first love and for us to remain in His love no matter what. God wants us to devote to Him the best portion of our time, attention, and love each day so we can be effective, refreshed people of joy.

My mornings are precious to me because it is often the only time I have entirely to myself. The rest of the day is spent dealing with the tyranny of the urgent in caring for my compromised elderly parents and other family needs. Since my morning hours are limited, I often feel torn between writing, exercising, or spending time reading the Scriptures and seeking the Lord's direction in prayer. However, when I put God first, He helps me serve my family with patience and love. He inspires my writing and stretches my productive hours in the day. Amy Carmichael once said, "You can always give without loving, but you can never love without giving."[3] I find that when I hurry through or shorten my time with the Lord, my day does not go as well because my heart has not been spiritually softened. Filling up with Christ's love, truth, and grace each day helps me to serve others in a loving manner. I need to do just as Matthew 6:33 (ESV) says to do: "But seek first the kingdom of God and his righteousness, and all these things will be added to you."

What if you have fallen short of putting God first in your life? Join the club of countless men and women, including those in the biblical "Hall of Faith" found in the book of Hebrews. We all have fallen short by putting relationships, dreams, ministry, family, jobs, and goals above our personal devotion to God. However, displacement of our heart's affection is not the end of our story. The good news is there is hope and redemption because of the gospel. Thank you, Jesus! Where there is authentic repentance and humility, there is also forgiveness and grace. God's grace is sufficient.

When we ask the Lord in prayer to restore our relationship with Him, He will take us into a deeper level of trust, adoration, and dependence. He will help us overcome our disappointments and fill our internal cup to overflowing with love, joy, and peace. When we are touched by God's lavish grace in a fresh way, it deepens our humility and softens us to the pain and brokenness of others. Only then will we become greater instruments of God's truth and grace.

I will never forget the day I was working on my computer in my Chicago apartment when, out of the blue, God took me completely off guard, whispering, *Do you love me?*

I sat back in my chair, and replied, "Of course I love you, Lord."

He replied, *Then trust me and open up your hands.*

God was preparing me to open up my hands and let go of a church ministry I had poured everything into for years. I thought, *Really, Lord? Are you honestly asking me to give all this up? We are finally about to move into a new building in the heart of the city, which has been a dream for several decades. Why now?*

I wanted to receive confirmation, so I prayed daily about this heartbreaking decision during the Lenten season. Thankfully, the

Lord gave me absolute clarity about taking this dramatic leap of faith the day after Easter Sunday. Even though I stepped into the decision faithfully, my heart and emotions still needed to catch up to my obedience. It was a process of letting go by peeling back one finger at a time until I fully released my grip. It was only after I opened up my hand in full surrender and resigned from my full-time ministry job that I realized God was also asking me to let go of my church home. Then, my Chicago home. The decision to let go was excruciating, but I had to remind myself that God does everything out of a heart of love for us. It felt like a triple heartbreak to say goodbye to my Chicago home, church ministry, and daily life with close friends . . . to follow Christ for a calling and destination unknown. I know the Lord wants our obedience more than our sacrifice (1 Samuel 15:22), so I trusted Him and stepped out in faith.

Often when we step out in total obedience to God's leading, Satan sees our vulnerability and tries to derail our destiny. Before the shipwreck of my life, many things collided at once. I felt like a small boat being storm-tossed and battered in the middle of the giant sea of chaos. During that season, I was hit with raging waves of physical health issues, false rumors, compounded grief, friendship betrayal, isolation, and lack of a loving community. It was a perfect storm, and I was feeling emotionally shipwrecked from being battered on all sides.

In the middle of all the devastation, the Lord reminded me of the countless, miraculous ways He had provided throughout my lifetime. This time of remembrance reassured me I could continue to trust in His

The decision to let go was excruciating, but I had to remind myself that God does everything out of a heart of love for us.

goodness and faithfulness for the future. As hard as it was, I held on to the promise of God's love and His good plans for my life. Upon reflection of God's deep love for me, my thoughts drifted back to a faith-strengthening experience that had taken place in Israel four years prior.

Crushed for a Purpose

During my trip to Israel with my Chicago church, we visited a place called the Scripture Gardens that depicted life in ancient Israel during the first and second centuries. Our guide was an amazing woman named Effie, who brought to life the rich, spiritual dimension of everyday Jewish culture. About halfway through the tour, she showed us an olive press display while explaining the multiple-press process to produce oil. Each time the olives were pressed, another rock weight would be placed at the end of the wooden lever. There was a trench around the bottom to collect the precious oil. The pure oil separated and rose to the top and all the impurities fell to the bottom.

The first pressing produced the best olive oil, which was used for the temple and ceremonial purposes to fill the menorah lamps and to anoint kings and people set apart for special service. Our holy God deserves the absolute best of our first fruits, so it makes sense that the first press would be given to Him as a proper sacrifice. The second olive press was for cooking, the third for oil lamps, and the fourth was used to make soap. We know that olive oil was also used for medicinal purposes, as noted in the parable of the good Samaritan, when the Samaritan bathed the man's wounds with olive oil before bandaging them so they would heal (Luke 10:34). After Effie explained the actual process for crushing olives and making olive oil, she said the best olive oil comes from fruit that has grown and matured for *forty years*. Thank you, Lord, for your unexpected encouragement that the best fruit is yet to come!

With lingering reflective thoughts about Effie's words, I turned and was faced with an image that left me breathless. Right in front of me was a crucifix made from an olive tree, which was only about a foot taller than the average height of a man. Effie explained that a crucifix used during the first and second centuries was not twenty feet high as portrayed in our current movies and modern paintings. Crucifixes were cut from olive trees, which grew about as wide as they were tall. The person crucified would be just about eye level to the scoffers who passed them by along the road. The crucified ones were often spit upon, ridiculed, and shamed, while dying a very public and painful death.

As I gazed upon the olive tree cross before me, I reflected on the way that Jesus died. He was not hanging high in the sky far away from His tormentors. No, they were right there in His face. Jesus was close enough to smell their sour breath as they sneered and mocked Him with taunting words, "If you are the King of the Jews, save yourself!" (Luke 23:37 NIV).

I imagined His head, dripping with blood from the crown of thorns, sinking lower under the weight of the shame, pain, exhaustion, and the sin of the world. My heart began to hurt as tears formed in my eyes, and I whispered, "Thank you, Jesus. I'm so undeserving of your sacrifice, and yet I'm so thankful."

Effie's voice caught my attention, and my thoughts returned to her as I heard her say, "If you asked Jesus today, *Do you really love me?*" There was a pause, and Effie stepped up on the rock next to the olive tree crucifixion and opened her arms to parallel the wooden cross. She flattened herself against the cross while facing us and said, "Jesus would probably open His outstretched arms and say, *I love you* this *much.*" She demonstrated Christ's position as He hung on the cross. That broke me, and the tears flowed down my cheeks as I wept.

I had come into a personal relationship with Jesus and was transformed by the Holy Spirit at seven years old, but I still intermittently struggled with really feeling loved by God, especially when dealing with exceedingly difficult life circumstances and people. It is common to feel unloved when we are emotionally wounded. But at that moment, I realized I had been viewing God's love through the lens of my own pain and loss, not knowing how to make sense of it. I had the wrong glasses on! God clarified my vision and showed me that I must always view my painful circumstances through the lens of the cross so I will never doubt His love again. Christ, with His nail-pierced hands and outstretched arms, demonstrated He loves me *this* much, and He loves you *this* much.

I stood there for a long time. When the others had left, I stood up on the rock and touched the place where Jesus's face would have been and spread my arms wide to touch the places where His nail-pierced hands would have been placed. I whispered, "I love you, too, Jesus, *this* much."

Our church group made our way into the room where we shared a traditional Jewish seder. Effie's soft voice did not diminish the power and potency of her inspired words. She illuminated the depth of God's love for us in every detail of the seder and how Christ fulfilled all the Old Testament promises. Effie's love for Jesus glowed radiantly from her sweet face, and she interspersed her teaching with hallelujah praises to our heavenly Father. The presence of the Holy Spirit was almost palpable in the room, and tears flowed again down my face as she spoke about the tenderness of our Lord. Effie looked at everything through the lens of God's love, and her ministry was powerful and healing. Scripture fell from her lips like pearls of truth draped over us like garments of praise and adoration.

At one point, she reached out and held my tearstained face with both hands and smiling radiantly said, "Jesus loves you." You could have heard a pin drop in the room, and my heart overflowed with His love. The tears continued down my cheeks as she taught the rest of the seder. Effie called it a reconciliation meal. She beautifully explained each portion of the meal and how it has been fulfilled in Christ. At the end, she encouraged us to prepare a meal for someone whom we have not spoken to for a long time and decide to forgive them as we have been forgiven. When we know that we are deeply forgiven and deeply loved, we are compelled to pass that grace and forgiveness on to those around us.

It was a profound night as I was able to extend another layer of forgiveness to my ex-husband for what emotionally felt like an incurable internal wound. Even though I had already forgiven him, there was another layer of forgiveness that still needed to be released. His destructive choices took so much away from me, leaving lasting scars on my ability to trust. The deeper you love someone, the more profoundly they can hurt you. However, God's love makes all things new again and heals any wound. It was an unexplainable movement of the Holy Spirit in my heart that released years of heartbreak, and my understanding of Christ's love grew deeper throughout the biblical tour of Israel.

God's truth from 2 Corinthians 4:8–9 (NIV) says, "We are hard pressed on every side, but not crushed; perplexed, but not in despair; persecuted, but not abandoned; struck down, but not destroyed." The Lord allowed me to survive the devastating loss of my marriage and propelled me into a different ministry calling I would have never chosen for myself. I'm so grateful that God allowed me to be crushed for a purpose but not permanently broken.

Brighter Days Ahead

Recalling God's unfailing love and faithfulness in the past will renew your hope for the future. Holding on to a shred of faith keeps you moving forward with believing hope that brighter days are ahead.

During one of my quiet times on the dock at Lake Titus, I noticed a small spruce tree that was only three feet tall on the shoreline. I wondered how this delicate little tree could make it through the harsh Adirondack winters with the shifting ice whose strength can tear out docks. I wondered if this little sapling would survive.

Years later, I noticed this same tree had not only survived the fierce Adirondack storms and strong winds, but it had thrived with abundant growth. The tree now stands straight as an arrow and is one of the healthiest trees on the water's edge. The Scripture passage came to mind:

> Therefore everyone who hears these words of mine and puts them into practice is like a wise man who built his house on the rock. The rain came down, the streams rose, and the winds blew and beat against that house; yet it did not fall, because it had its foundation on the rock. But everyone who hears these words of mine and does not put them into practice is like a foolish man who built his house on sand. (Matthew 7:24–26 NIV)

My family was founded upon the rock of Jesus Christ. Because of that truth, we have not only survived the many storms of life, but we have persevered and thrived despite hardships because Christ has been our strength, our rock, and our firm foundation.

We must anticipate that God is going to move in a mighty way in our current circumstances because of His great love for us. The Lord will not only heal our wounds but will redeem them for His glory as well. Every sorrow, every tear, and every loss can be repurposed for the glory of God. I felt that way about my divorce. You can imagine my surprise when God called me to work at a large church in the care ministry and one of my jobs was to lead DivorceCare groups. God works for good in all things when we open our hands and trust Him.

While I was recuperating in the Adirondacks, I was reminded of countless stories of God's faithfulness as I sat alone on the red bench in front of Donnelly's eating my ice cream. I fondly recalled a fun "auntie day" from the previous summer with my three nieces. It was a hot day in July, and we decided it would be fun to take an adventurous road trip together. It is an hour-long drive through the Adirondack Mountains to Donnelly's Soft Serve Ice Cream Shack in Saranac Lake, New York, but entirely worth the trip. On the way there, we made up lyrics and sang silly songs about our endless love for Donnelly's ice cream, which made the time go by faster.

Anticipation is a great feeling as you look forward to something with every fiber in your being. Your blood starts pumping, your mouth starts salivating, and your stomach begins to growl. You cannot *wait* to have the frosty taste of frozen cream melting in your mouth. The anticipation is half the fun! I asked the girls, "What flavor do you think it will be today?" and they screamed out their favorite choices and begged me to buy them a bigger-sized cone than their parents would approve of. It is fun being an auntie, one of life's greatest blessings.

The Adirondack countryside is stunningly beautiful, and right before going down the hill that takes you to Donnelly's is one of the most spectacular views in Saranac Lake. There is a panoramic glimpse of the forty-six High Peaks mountains all around you, and their majesty is simply breathtaking. Below the mountains, the open green pastures are dotted with yellow goldenrod and orange paintbrush wildflowers, with round hay wheels artistically scattered throughout the fields. The old brown barn in the distance nicely balances the dark blue mountains in contrast to the green-, yellow-, and orange-painted fields. God's artistic fingerprints can be seen all over His Adirondack creation. I think Claude Monet would surely have stopped here to paint *plein air* to capture the raw beauty of the "forever wild" mountains.

After we passed by this delightful visual feast of divine beauty, we drove over the crest of the hill, and there in all its white and shining splendor was Donnelly's Soft Serve Ice Cream Shack! As the sun glistened off the white dairy barn, you could almost hear a hallelujah choir lifting their voices in perfect harmony. The girls squealed with delight, and the car accelerated going down the hill like a horse bound for home, knowing the best is yet to come.

We took the last parking spot, ran to the sugar shack, and found out the one flavor offering for the day was vanilla with a strawberry twist. My youngest niece was thrilled because pink is her favorite color. She loves all things pink. After we got our cones, there was contented silence as we eagerly devoured them so as not to lose a drop of the creamy cold goodness. I describe it as party-in-your-mouth good to indicate the highest form of taste-bud pleasure.

I can still remember it like it was just yesterday. The setting was perfect as we sat on the red bench outside the shack, leaning against the flower boxes overflowing with red geraniums and purple and white pansies, and smiling at the long line of hungry patrons. I was filled with joy as I watched my giggling nieces happily licking their ice cream cones while swinging their legs under the red bench with carefree bliss. I will savor the sweetness of this memory forever. It is permanently etched in my mind. We gazed off into the distance, looking at a beautiful landscape, Whiteface Mountain playing center stage with its distinctive white scar cascading sideways down its face. There was no need for words as the moment was simply perfect being together, enjoying ice cream, and admiring God's creation.

As I sat there, remembering that day, a truck drove by, and the sound of the engine brought me back from that joyful memory to my present sorrow. I smiled through my sadness as I reflected on those happier and simpler days, and I prayed that the Lord would restore the years that had been lost. I believed with unwavering faith that God would restore more to me than what had been taken away. "Weeping may last through the night, but joy comes in the morning" (Psalm 30:5 NLT). During seasons of sadness in our lives, it is important to remind ourselves that we are fully loved by God, and we will experience everlasting joy in eternity.

The more you invest in people and places, the more it can feel like a part of you dies on the inside when they are gone. The deeper your loyalty, the greater you feel the loss. Have you experienced the pain of divorce, the loss of a special friendship, moved your home to another state, or resigned from a job you loved? I have experienced these losses in life and many more. Through it all, Jesus has walked with me through the grieving process. Grief is a powerful emotion that can bring you into the depth of intense sadness, but I want to assure you that life will get better, and the Lord will help you climb out of this pit of despair. Whenever we feel as if nobody understands, loves, or cares, we can rest in the fact that Jesus loves us dearly. He will always be close by our side when we seek His face.

Life Lessons Learned

The best way to begin to revive our dry bones is to immerse ourselves in the promises of God's Holy Word—His living water. Allowing God's Word to wash over us brings healing everywhere we are hurting. When we meditate on the promises of God and remind ourselves of His past and present faithfulness, He will renew our hope. God is faithful. He loves us dearly, and we can trust Him enough to surrender everything into His sovereign care. He wants to be our foundational rock in the storms of life so we can stand tall in the face of opposition. He is our calm in the chaos. As someone who is intimately familiar with suffering, Joni Eareckson Tada posted this on her Facebook page, "Suffering will always show me what I love—either the God of all comfort or the comfort that can become my god."⁴ Boy, isn't that the truth!

When we realize that it is more important to please God than it is to please others, we will experience a greater peace and clarity about our true priorities. We do not have to be perfect in order to be loved, for God loves us completely in our imperfection. There is nothing we can do to earn His love, and there is nothing we can do to lose it. There is no sweeter love than Christ's love for us, which makes it easier to turn away from our idols and return to our first love. Idols seek to distract our focus, divide our hearts, and rob us of authentic love.

Our true understanding of love comes when we begin to understand the depth of how much God loves us through the sacrifice of His only Son. The more we understand how much He loves us through His Word, the stronger our faith muscles will become when He asks us to surrender it all.

We do not have to be perfect in order to be loved, for God loves us completely in our imperfection. There is nothing more we can do to earn His love, and there is nothing we can do to lose it.

CLIMB THE MOUNTAIN
SCENE 2

The intensity of the morning sun created the illusion of diamonds sparkling on the waters. My paddle dipped into the brilliant, liquid sunlight as my kayak glided forward. There was not a single cloud in the clear blue sky. What a perfect day to hike to the top of Elephant's Head. I decided to access the private trail located at the water's edge. When I docked my kayak at South Beach, it evoked a sweet memory of my nieces when they were young. They renamed this area "Secret Beach" because they would sneak off on kayaking adventures with backpacks full of snacks and hang out on the beach with their friends.

Hoisting my kayak out of the water, I reminisced about the Lake Titus Breakfast Walk. The Breakfast Walk is an annual event when all the people who own camps around the lake head down in their boats to South Beach for food and fellowship. We use this time to catch up with each other while we wait in line for our breakfast, which cooks over a large griddle under a pine tree canopy. Our stomachs growl as the fragrance of the crispy bacon, fried eggs, and buttermilk pancakes waft under our noses and tickle our taste buds. As I recalled the past, the forest came alive with hearty laughter, joyful reunions, and tasty food. Right now, there is not a single soul at South Beach; only the memories linger in the air.

I spotted the Elephant's Head hiking path and quickly followed the orange dots on the trees. The jagged trail was newly marked but still overgrown with roots, rocks, and fallen tree branches. As I embarked on my adventure, I reflected on how this jagged path is a metaphor for the Christian life of sanctification and surrender. Like this winding trail, following Christ has not been a smooth journey because of unexpected detours and painful hardships.

Trust is a critical element to trailblazing. When I'm hiking a new trail and I don't know where I am going, I need to trust that the trail markers on the tree will lead me to the summit. In the same way, I need to trust in God's Word and the Holy Spirit's leading to light my path in the direction I should go. Sometimes God has asked me to move forward, and other times He has asked me to wait for His perfect timing. I remembered something Stormie Omartian said: "God doesn't often reveal the details of where He is taking us because He wants us to trust Him for every step."[1] Believing faith is a daily trust walk.

Over the years, I have had to wait on God's timing to resolve family issues, mend relationships, open doors for ministry, deal with injustices, heal a sick family member, and fulfill my deferred dreams, like publishing my first book. I know how frustrating it is to wait on God's timing when life is in total chaos. But through it all, I have learned that waiting on God is not passive, for it requires the Holy Spirit's self-control and strength to develop trust muscles through the waiting period. For it is "not by might, nor by power, but by my Spirit, says the Lord of Hosts" (Zechariah 4:6 ESV). Surrendering our will and plans often goes hand in hand with waiting on God.

I'll be totally honest with you. Waiting is not within my comfort zone! I have often felt like a racehorse caged in at the starting gate chomping on my bit ready to burst out of the starting gate. Running at a fast pace is what I have known all my life. Even when I am hiking, I enjoy sprinting up the mountain like a mountain goat.

> *Surrendering our will and plans often goes hand in hand with waiting on God.*

However, God slows me down so He can sanctify and redirect me. He cares more about my character than my comfort. It is counterintuitive for me to wait, but I choose to do so out of love for Christ and to trust in His sovereign plan.

As I continued hiking the jagged trail, my thoughts were being sanctified when I realized I was still holding on too tightly to my dreams. I had already laid down my plans and was waiting for God's perfect timing, but it seemed like an eternity passed as I waited . . . rested . . . waited . . . trusted . . . waited . . . worshiped . . . and waited some more. Once again, I humbly opened my hands and released my dream of being a writer into His outstretched hands and said, "It is your book, Lord, and I am writing it for you. Do with it what you wish." I had finally settled in my heart that I never needed to publish it. You see, the Lord is bringing renewed hope and healing to me both through the process of writing the book and digging deeper into God's healing Word. Perhaps this is His sovereign plan.

Just then, God interrupted my train of thought and surprised me when I heard in my spirit, "Not now doesn't mean never. Trust me with the process, for I am with you."

CHAPTER 2

CLIMBING THE JAGGED TRAIL

And calling the crowd to him with his disciples, he said
to them: "If anyone would come after me, he must deny
himself and take up his cross and follow me."

Mark 8:34 ESV

Trust Walk

Before I left Chicago, I knew I was at a crossroads decision. I could either lay down the years of emotional pain into the loving hands of Jesus, or I could clench my fists and grow bitter over all the injustices incurred. After going for a prayer walk on the university campus, I stood in front of the larger-than-life, nine-foot-tall stone sculpture of Jesus in front of the chapel, and I slipped my hand inside Jesus's large open hand. My hand looked so small compared to His. I whispered a pivotal prayer. "I surrender all of the pain, suffering, and disappointments to you, Lord, and I trust you will bring about vindication and healing in your timing." I was leaving Chicago, closing a significant chapter in my life, and I didn't want to carry the heavy burdens into my next chapter in New England.

I knew that trusting God and surrendering my plans for His greater one would come with a cost. Even though I felt as though I was giving up everything, in reality I would have everything to gain. As we draw close to God in surrender, He plants a redemptive dream in our hearts that is often birthed through second chances and new beginnings. God's timing is perfect. The cost of surrendering involves giving up our pride, our disappointments, and sometimes our dreams. However, this is not the end of our stories. As we draw close to the Lord, He turns our pride into peaceful humility, our plans into a powerful kingdom purpose, and our dreams into a God-given calling.

As we draw close to the Lord, He turns our pride into peaceful humility, our plans into a powerful kingdom purpose, and our dreams into a God-given calling.

Surrender is an *all-in* decision. We can't sort of surrender or partially trust. I love this quote by Karen Goodman: "If you try to surrender just a little bit to God, He will know. It is like trying to carry on a conversation with someone who is preoccupied with the newspaper [or cell phone]; which is most unsatisfying and practically useless."[1] When we talk about total surrender, the best place to look is in the Scriptures. The Bible is full of people who trusted God and surrendered their lives to follow Him. Jesus asked His disciples to give up their comfortable lives, professions, and homes to follow Him to a destination unknown.

One day, Jesus was walking along the shore of the Sea of Galilee when He saw two brothers named Simon (later renamed Peter) and Andrew. As described in Matthew 4:18–19, Jesus called out to them, "Come, follow me, and I will show you how to fish for people!" They dropped their fishing nets immediately and followed Jesus to become His disciples. The men whom Jesus called to be his disciples came from various backgrounds and most had unsavory reputations. But Jesus saw their teachable hearts, called them into ministry, and trained them along the way. Each disciple learned what it meant to trust Jesus and completely surrender his life for the sake of the kingdom.

It fascinates me that none of the disciples Jesus chose were religious. They were not Pharisees, Levites, or rabbis, the kind of men who were deemed godly by religious standards during the first century. Jesus did not choose the religious men because their hearts were so hard they could not recognize the Son of the living God standing before them. Instead, Jesus picked men with soft, teachable hearts; that included feisty fishermen, two guys known as "sons of thunder" because of their tempers, and a tax collector who was viewed by society as someone betraying his own people by working for Rome. The motley crew also included a doubter, a betrayer, and several others. These were imperfect people. But Jesus saw into their hearts and knew which ones would be willing to surrender their lives to follow Him. God knows all your weaknesses and imperfections, but He still wants to use you as His ambassador to reach the lost. Are you willing to give up everything to follow Jesus? Is there anything you are holding too tightly?

Jesus made it clear that following Him is costly, but His grace is a free gift to us. The key is we need to *receive* His gospel grace, *apply* His gospel grace, and *share* His gospel grace with others. It is not enough to only know about the gospel in our minds. The Lord wants the gospel message to transform our heads, hearts, and hands. Giving up our plans, goals, habits, and reputation to humbly follow Jesus requires denying ourselves daily so Jesus can have greater prominence.

"And calling the crowd to him with his disciples, he said to them: 'If anyone would come after me, he must deny himself and take up his cross and follow me'" (Mark 8:34 ESV). The people who were willing to follow Jesus recognized His voice and immediately responded. They did not weigh the pros and cons, nor did they assemble a committee to get a group consensus. They simply recognized the Lord's voice and dropped everything to follow Him. "My sheep listen to My voice, and I know them, and they follow Me" (John 10:27 NASB). When Christ's voice prompts us to follow Him, out of loving obedience we can respond with complete surrender, knowing we can trust Him as our guide.

Full surrender allows us to take a journey on the jagged path of sanctification, which will refine our character. The Lord gently takes off our filthy rags of sin, then gives us His royal robes of righteousness so we can become more like Christ. "There are many who have accepted Christ as their Lord, but have never yet come to the final, absolute surrender of everything."[2] If you have never experienced a trust walk of full surrender—now is the time. Our Savior will walk with you, give you His spiritual gear, and show you how to make good decisions that will honor Him.

Our trust walk of faith will not be a smooth path. It is more like a jagged trail we must climb that leads us through peaks and valleys, over boulders, and across suspended rope bridges. Henry Cloud and John Townsend said it this way: "Trust is the bridge over the raging river. Trust is how we access God's way for us. Trust is acting on your behalf that God will make a way. You will never benefit from your faith in God until you step on the bridge and start walking across. Trust is both an attitude and an action."[3] Surrender is not a onetime decision; it is a thousand choices to lay down our own plans and trust God's plans above our own.

This is particularly challenging to do especially for driven, goal-oriented people. This world's perilous path is filled with unexpected traps and snares. Sometimes we trip, fall on our faces, or worse, break a leg. But the good news is that we have Jesus as our mountain guide. He is the only One with the reliable compass, tools, and knowledge to navigate the trail to surrender. He will lead us through the narrow path. He will never abandon us just because we have fallen and broken a few bones. The Lord is patient with us, takes time to bandage our wounds, and helps us get back on our feet. Jesus sees into our hearts, knows our potential, and has a unique purpose and plan for each of us. He does not throw us away because we have made poor choices or are banged up by life circumstances.

> *Surrender is not a onetime decision; it is a thousand choices to lay down our own plans and trust God's plans above our own.*

Jesus delights in reaching and redeeming wounded soldiers for Christ. Amy Carmichael said, "Soldiers may be wounded in battle and sent to a hospital. A hospital isn't a shelf. It's a place of repair. And a soldier in the spiritual army is never off his battlefield. He is only removed to another part of the battlefield when a wound interrupts what he was meant to do, and sets him doing something else."[4] Whether our wounds are caused by someone else or by our own bad choices, Jesus desires to heal and redeem our painful experiences. "We are made right with God by placing our faith in Jesus Christ. And this is true for everyone who believes, no matter who we are or where we have been. For everyone has sinned; we all fall short of God's glorious standard" (Romans 3:22–23 NLT). While God's forgiveness is astonishing, we should never take His costly grace for granted. Our redemption cost His only Son, Jesus, His very life!

> *To be redeemed is to be rescued.*

Redeemed Followers

To be redeemed is to be rescued. Because of Christ, we are rescued from our sin and forgiven of our failures. It is a glorious privilege to be given a fresh start; a blank canvas. This quote by Roy Lessin really says it all: "When the Bible says that you have been redeemed, it means that you have been absolutely freed, fully released, and totally delivered from all that had you bound in the past."[5] Christ sacrificed His life so we could gain new life and follow Him. The apostle Peter highlights God's lavish mercy, radical transformation, and His ultimate redemptive plan.

Peter, who was full of courage and foolish naïveté, followed Jesus proudly. Peter was not the perfect Christian by any stretch of the imagination, but he earnestly followed Jesus despite his faults. What God desires from us is a teachable heart and a willingness to change. Peter's heart was in the right place, but he often missed the mark. Nevertheless, Jesus was patient with Peter's poor timing, inaccurate statements, bold declarations, and denials. He never gave up on Peter. In the same way, Jesus never gives up on us, despite our poor performance, nasty attitudes, and ill-spoken words. Even after Peter denied his Lord three times, the risen Jesus redeemed Peter's denial by asking him if he loved

Him. After Peter said three times, "Yes, Lord, you know I love you," Jesus said, "Then feed my sheep!" (John 21:15–17 NIV). Jesus wanted Peter to follow Him. He wants to use our failures and redeem them for God's kingdom purposes.

Peter tasted the goodness of Jesus's grace and forgiveness; his passion was rekindled to share the gospel again. He knew spreading the good news was the ultimate purpose and focus for his life. The Lord was with Peter through the power of the Holy Spirit, and thousands became Christ followers through his preaching (Acts 2:41 NLT). Peter's boldness in preaching the gospel resulted in him being thrown in jail. Even when the situation looked grim for Peter, the power of prayer empowered the angel of the Lord to actively work on Peter's behalf to release him.

"Suddenly, there was a bright light in the cell, and an angel of the Lord stood before Peter. The angel struck him on the side to awaken him and said, 'Quick! Get up!' And the chains fell off his wrists. Then the angel told him, 'Get dressed and put on your sandals.' And he did. 'Now put on your coat and follow me,' the angel ordered" (Acts 12:7–8 NLT). The angel broke the chains off his arms and miraculously led Peter safely out of prison. Time and time again, the Lord provided for Peter as he walked in obedience to share the good news.

Jesus redeemed Peter's life in such a radical way. Upon repentance, Christ took Peter's fearful denial and transformed Peter into a bold preacher to save thousands of souls. When the Lord calls us to follow Him through impossible situations, He always makes a way. Nothing is impossible for God, and that is why denying ourselves, picking up our crosses, and following Jesus is an adventure filled with modern-day miracles and answered prayers. Are you like Peter, someone who is ready to get off the sidelines and embark on an adventure that will knock your merino wool hiking socks off? Let's go!

In Christ's Strength

When we are at our lowest point, we can depend on Christ's strength to see us through. Bruce Wilkinson said, "The same power that raised

Jesus from the dead is available to lift you up out of your private pit."[6] At this moment, some might feel fired up for an adventure with Jesus, ready and raring to go while others might be feeling afraid, exhausted, or too beaten down. In either case, here are the questions to ask: Have you been carrying a heavy burden in your backpack that is draining your strength and slowing you down? What is God asking you to surrender? What would the cost be? You might be thinking, *Well, I don't want to give up everything and suffer like the disciples did.* Let me assure you, this world is filled with suffering and pain that we cannot escape or avoid. Joseph Stowell said, "For those of us who know God, pain is a process with a certain purpose. We don't make it through tough times. We are *made through* tough times—made into the beauty of Christ Jesus. And in that perspective, the pain is worth the gain."[7] Thankfully, Jesus promises to be with us through the painful refining process.

Jesus blazes a trail through the thick forest and lights the path that we should follow. He is with us always, and He reminds us of His unfailing love and limitless strength. I can't imagine what my life would be like without Jesus. It is only because of Jesus that I can continue to stand tall after being beaten down by excruciating trials. Jesus gave me the strength to press on when I was weak and pointed me in the right direction with every new trail that crossed my path.

Trusting God empowers us to shake off our defeated posture, stand tall, and walk victoriously. We don't have to fear the unknown. We need to remind ourselves, "Fear disrupts our faith and becomes the biggest obstacle to trusting and obeying God."[8] We have a choice to trust God and stand firm in our faith. When you trust someone completely, you don't have to fear, for as Scripture tells us, "There is no fear in love. Perfect love drives out fear" (1 John 4:18 NASB). Fear weighs us down and holds us back from living fully. By contrast, God's love empowers us. The Lord knows us, loves us, and has a special plan for our lives that He ordained when He knit us together in our mother's womb (Psalm 139:13–16). God knows us in our innermost being, and He has a wonderful future in store.

We all have seasons of wandering in the barren wilderness. It is in those desolate times when we especially long to be in the promised land where life is joyful and abundant. During wilderness seasons, we need to let our faith be bigger than our fears (John 14:27). When Joshua brought the Israelites out of the desert they had wandered in for forty years, God commanded them, "Be strong and courageous! Do not be afraid or discouraged. For the Lord your God is with you wherever you go" (Joshua 1:9 NLT). God had prepared Joshua to lead the Israelites into the promised land. Even though there were plenty of doubters and opposition, God gave Joshua the strength to follow through on the difficult task before him. God will do the same for me and for you. I would much rather face life's challenges with Christ's strength than without it. Wouldn't you? Before we embark on an exhilarating life-changing adventure, we need to lay down our fears and burdens so we can travel light and unhindered.

Lay Down Your Burdens

With tears in His eyes, Jesus is reaching out to you and asking you to take His hand. He wants to lift the heavy backpack that is weighing you down. Jesus speaks to us in a soothing, low voice,

> My child, come to me, I can see the weariness in your eyes, and I long to give you rest in my arms. Won't you lay down your burdens before me and let me carry them for you? Sit with me awhile and let me teach you my ways. You don't need to worry or be afraid. I am humble and gentle, and I promise you will find encouragement, hope, and rest for your weary soul. You are not alone. I'll take on your burdens from here so you will feel lighter, and I will fill you with my hope and a promise of a new life. (Matthew 11:28–30, paraphrase mine)

God wants to give you the peace, rest, and strength, you desire. You don't have to clean up your life before you come to Him. He wants to remove your shame, anxiety, and fears. You can be totally honest with God because He loves you and knows everything already. Pray with me right now and make a commitment to Christ for the first time or recommit to Him.

> *Lord*, I trust You completely as my Lord and Savior, and I want to follow You all the days of my life. I lay down all my heavy burdens at the foot of the cross. Please forgive me of all my sin, pride, and rebellion in my heart. I desire to do things Your way, Lord. I believe that Jesus is the Son of God, He died on the cross for my sins, and God raised Him from the dead. Lord, I know it is by believing the gospel truth in my heart that I am made right with You. Your Word says, "If you openly declare that Jesus is Lord and believe in your heart that God raised him from the dead, you will be saved" (Romans 10:9 NLT). Thank you, Lord, for helping me be a new (or renewed) creation in Christ Jesus. Create a clean heart in me. I invite the Holy Spirit to indwell me to be my counselor, comforter, and source of wisdom. Praise You, Lord, I love You. Amen.

As you spend some time alone in silent prayer to let the meaning of these words wash over you, you might feel the weight immediately lift from your heart, or it might take a little while to live into the truth of what was just accomplished for you. You just accepted a free gift of grace and forgiveness. Hallelujah!

At this very moment, I want you to know deep in your soul that you are accepted, known, and loved by God completely. When we come to the Lord with genuine repentance, our sins are forgiven. Scripture says, "He removes our sins as far as the east is from the west" (Psalm 103:12 NLT). God doesn't remember your sins anymore, and He will never haunt you or taunt you with your past. There are times when the Holy Spirit will convict us to make the bold steps of asking for forgiveness or making amends for wrongdoing. However, if you are constantly reminded of all your failures, that is the voice of Satan, the accuser, condemning you. Don't listen to that voice as it will only drag you down into a dark hole of despair.

My family and I went to the top of Whiteface Mountain, which overlooks the Adirondack Park and several other mountain ranges and lakes. The breathtaking view makes the steep climb worth every grueling step. After we took photos at the summit and enjoyed our picnic lunch, we decided to go down the mountain via the elevator (yes, there is an elevator there!) so we could save time and enjoy the quaint town of Lake Placid.

In 1929, Franklin D. Roosevelt was inspired to build Veterans Memorial Highway, which winds its way around Whiteface Mountain. However, the road stops just three hundred feet short of the top. Thankfully, provisions were made to carve out the center of the mountain for the installation of an elevator to make the peak wheelchair accessible for people who are elderly and disabled. How wonderful to be able to enjoy the vista with wind in their hair and the unparalleled views of the forty-six High Peaks all around them. It is an exhilarating experience to be at the summit of the fifth highest peak in the Adirondack Mountains.

At the top of Whiteface Mountain, the gatekeeper, an older man, opened the gate for the crowd. Everyone crammed inside the old-fashioned elevator; then he closed the gate and pulled the lever for our descent. I thought it was strange that he was dressed in a winter jacket with gloves and a hat in the middle of the hot summer, but I would soon understand the reason. The elevator shaft was gored out of the mountain rock, and the temperature began to get colder and colder as we descended. *A warm winter coat and hat would feel pretty good right now,* I thought as I smiled at the gatekeeper. Moisture from the mountain spring water dripped down the rock, making it feel even colder. Damp coldness permeated our bones, and we couldn't wait to see the light of day. I couldn't help but think, *What if this archaic elevator gets stuck or breaks down?* I shivered at the thought. Everyone was silent as the elevator plummeted downward at a rate that made our ears pop; we wanted to get the ride over with as soon as possible.

Despair is like being in an elevator that has plunged you into a dark and damp space with no exit and no end to your misery. The longer you are in the shaft of despair, the harder it is to remember the warmth and sunshine of the summit you enjoyed minutes ago. Exit the elevator! Come out and see the light of day again. Sometimes we can be our own worst enemies as we beat ourselves up and rehearse all the pain, suffering, and failures of the past. It is important to believe and accept that Christ's grace is sufficient to cover *all* of our sins once and for all. We need to remind ourselves of what is true based on God's Word: "For once you were full of darkness, but now you have light from the Lord. So, live as people of the light" (Ephesians 5:8). God's truth will expose the darkness of the oppressive lies so we can begin to heal and have hope again. However, "You must know the truth in order for the truth to deliver you."[9]

The truth is each one of us is a beautiful, new creation in Christ. When God looks at you and me, He sees the righteousness, purity, and blamelessness of His Son. John MacArthur said it well: "It is important for every Christian to keep in mind the great difference between his position and his practice, his standing and his state. God sees us as righteous, because He sees us through His righteous Son, who has taken our place, and because He has planted in us a righteous new nature."[10] The Holy Spirit has been deposited into our hearts to help us live out our new nature, pick up our cross, and follow Him.

Christ-followers are always cross-bearers.

Your Cross Stories

Christ-followers are always cross-bearers. It was a significant moment for me when I realized on a deeper level that Christ-followers and cross-bearers are inextricably linked together. Jesus guided his disciples and us to do the same (Mark 8:34). Following Christ means to pick up our heavy cross of suffering and persevere. We cannot stay in the pit of despair; we need to pick up our cross, keep moving, and climb the mountain in front of us.

Each of us has a cross to bear, and each person has unique circumstances. Mercifully, we have been given the Lord's strength and assistance to carry our cross of heartache. Perhaps you had a child who died an early death, you have a physical disability that limits you to a wheelchair, or your business venture failed, and you lost everything. There are many kinds of crosses that people carry—consequences of our sin, suffering from someone else's sinful choices, or hardships we have endured. As you carry your cross, let your cross shape you and sanctify you into Christ's image. Do not be afraid or ashamed of your cross. Your cross story makes you more humbly dependent upon His grace and grateful for His sacrifice. His astonishing grace motivates us to share the goodness of Jesus with others.

> Anitha Jabastion wrote a beautiful story about a boy who desperately wanted to meet Christ. He was praying hard about it. One day, the Lord told him to walk up the mountain carrying his cross. He took his cross and began his journey. In some time, he began to feel the heaviness of the cross. He cut out a small portion of it and began to walk. Soon after, he still felt the cross was too heavy. He again cut out another portion and continued his journey. This happened a few more times till he finally reached the mountain top. There, he found Jesus standing at the peak of another neighboring mountain. Jesus told him, "My son, now lay down your cross and walk over to me." But as he laid down his cross, he found that it could not bridge the two mountains. The gap was exactly the same size that he had cut off his cross. He realized that had he managed to bear the cross without cutting it down, he would have reached Jesus.[11]

The boy's effort to cut off part of his cross was like trying to cut off part of his testimony and take credit for his own success of climbing his mountain. However, it is carrying the weight of our cross stories that helps us to recognize our need for a Savior. We cannot achieve salvation through our own efforts and strength. Our cross humbles us and points us to the only One who can save us.

Our cross stories enhance our personal testimonies. Part of my cross story is the broken dream of being a wife and mother. Sadly, I experienced two miscarriages during my marriage. Every time someone asks me if I have children, there is a small twinge of pain that touches my shattered dream.

As you carry your cross, let your cross shape you and sanctify you into Christ's image.

However, the Lord has redeemed my desire to nurture and help people grow through various ministry and discipleship opportunities. The loss of not being able to have physical children was redeemed with the joy of investing in spiritual children. Isaiah 54:1 promises the woman who has never given birth will have more children than the woman who has a husband. I have hidden this promise in my heart and discovered the joy in its meaning. Each time I cling to God's promises, He helps me to see my situation through His perspective. I trust Jesus with this piece and many other pieces of my cross story.

In Christ's strength, we can pick up our cross of shattered dreams and press on toward the high calling we have in Jesus Christ, knowing Jesus makes all the difference. *Without* Jesus, we would be crushed and overwhelmed under the weight of our cross. *With* Jesus, we can be victorious overcomers. There is a redemptive thread the Lord has stitched through the fabric of our life, and He uses all the pieces of our story to make a beautiful and colorful tapestry.

At the Fletcher Allen Hospital in Burlington, Vermont, there is a large wall sculpture that extends from the third floor all the way down to the lobby. At the top of the sculpture is an antique black sewing machine that has the words *"Fabric of Life"* etched in white in old-fashioned lettering on the side. The fabric hanging off the sewing machine is constructed from several sheets of copper that have been cut into squares and then artistically stitched together. The color of each square is either an oxidized green, brushed warm copper, or a mahogany brown. The sheets of different colored copper look like waves of fabric cascading down several floors to the lobby area. I thought about the thousands of lives that come through the doors of the hospital.

Every life has a story, and our stories are interwoven together by the Master Weaver to create an intricate tapestry.

Our Creator uses every piece of our stories, whether it is bright and shiny or old and oxidized. So, what is your cross story? God often uses our cross story as part of our ministry calling to reach hurting people around us. For example, if your spouse has passed away, you can use your cross story to identify and comfort other widows. Perhaps you have overcome an eating disorder or a different addiction; you can help others be set free by leading a Christ-centered care group.

I have been the primary caregiver for my two parents for over a decade and have seen them through many years of physical health issues, such as overcoming stage 4 cancer, heart issues, back issues, a broken femur, being wheelchair bound, septic gallbladder, detached retinas, memory issues, and so much more. I would never have known how challenging it would be to be a caregiver if I had not gone through it myself. My vast experiences have given me a profound understanding and compassion for other caregivers. Nothing in life is wasted, for God can redeem all our tears and all the lost years.

Our Redeemed Identity

Our cross does not define us, but the One who helps us carry our cross does. The world takes notice when we delight in the identity of our healer instead of despairing about our wounds. Instead of dwelling on past failures, we can refocus our thoughts on God's profound and undeserved forgiveness. As we begin to live out our new Christ-centered identity, we become living testaments of God's goodness and grace. Your identity in Christ has also given you a new family. "For you did not receive the spirit of slavery to fall back into fear, but you have received a Spirit of adoption as sons, by whom we cry, 'Abba! Father!' The Spirit himself testifies with our spirit that we are children of God" (Romans 8:15–16 ESV). You have been adopted as God's daughters and sons when you

Our cross does not define us, but the One who helps us carry our cross does.

accepted Christ as your Lord and Savior. When your mind begins to play the old, negative messages again, redirect your thoughts by reciting the Scriptures. Part of living in the freedom of God's truth is choosing to believe our new identity in Christ and not rehashing our destructive experiences or feelings.

Speaking God's truth out loud breaks the power of the lies. For example, if you are experiencing brokenness, then remind yourself of Isaiah 53:5 (NIV), which tells us, "By His wounds, we are healed." If you are feeling defeated by hurtful words hurled at you like arrows, speak out loud Romans 8:37 (NLT): "Overwhelming victory is ours through Christ, who

> *The world takes notice when we delight in the identity of our healer instead of despairing about our wounds.*

loved us." If fear is causing you to feel stuck, then memorize 2 Timothy 1:7 (NLT): "For God has not given us a spirit of fear and timidity, but of power, love, and self-discipline." We can choose to meditate on the truth of God's Word instead of focusing on our crippling fears. The "Wounded Identity vs. Redeemed Identity Chart" located at the end of the book in the appendix 1 will give you more tools on how to claim your redeemed identity.

Have you ever wanted to unplug from the outside world and stop all the noise? I vividly remember a season when I boldly did the unthinkable. I canceled my email, Facebook account, and all social media, and even got rid of my iPhone. I literally withdrew from all toxic input. The raw emotion surrounding my wounded identity caused me to create a safe place to heal through self-imposed isolation. Renewed hope was birthed through meditating on God's promises in His Word. I must have repeated this Scripture a thousand times: "Let us not become weary in doing good, for at the proper time we will reap a harvest if we do not give up" (Galatians 6:9 NIV). I held on to God's promise that there would be a great harvest at the end of my trial. Speaking this Scripture out loud gave me hope for the future and the strength to press on. The words you speak audibly will either confirm your faith in Christ or confirm your unbelief. It is essential to give a strong voice to God's truth from Scripture and meditate on its healing power. Philippians 4:8 (ESV) states, "Finally brothers, whatever is true, whatever is honorable, whatever is just, whatever is pure, whatever is lovely, whatever is commendable, if there is anything of excellence, if there is anything worthy of praise, think about these things." When we dwell on the truth of who we are in Christ, then we begin to embrace our new life, our new identity, and our new name.

Many years ago, when I was newly divorced and struggling with this new identity, I flew home to Connecticut to be with my family for Easter. My mother shared a rather profound and life-changing concept with me. She gently listened to the intense grief, anger, and shame I was feeling about my divorce and how I felt like I had a scarlet *D* tattooed on my forehead. Mom looked at me with a smile and said, "Sharon, it is time to give yourself a new name. Your name is not Divorced, and you are not defined by your wounds."

My curiosity was piqued, and she proceeded to read a devotional entitled "A New Name." The synopsis of the story was about a young man named Rodney who played tennis and had a slow serve and backhand. His coach decided to call Rodney "The Rocket." After years of training, believing, and living up to his new name, he became an outstanding professional tennis player with an incredibly fast serve. After my mom recounted the story, she smiled and suggested we pray for God to give me a new name. During our prayer time, the name the Lord placed on my heart was Victorious. By the grace of God, the power of Christ, and the guidance of the Holy Spirit, I *am* victorious.

God's Word came alive to me as I pondered the Scriptures about the Lord giving people new names. In the Bible, new names were symbolic of how God had changed men's and women's characters and hearts. It's interesting that all of these individuals' names were changed right before they were enlisted into kingdom service and given a covenant promise or a significant blessing. Abram became Abraham, Sarai became Sarah, Jacob became Israel, Simon became Peter, and Saul became Paul. They each endured a life-altering experience that became the catalyst for new life, new growth, and a new character. In many cultures, a name has special significance and meaning. First Samuel 25:25 (NKJV) states, "For as his name is, so is he," which means in the Hebrew tradition that a child's name expresses the character they will exhibit later in life.

The names we are called can be used to build us up or tear us down. Our Enemy whispers names of condemnation to oppress and discourage us to the point of believing the bad names are true. What do you call yourself? Is the name affirming and life-giving? Are you replaying failures in your head? Does the name line up with who you are as a child of the living God? It is critical to hold your thoughts captive when you start replaying negative names in your mind. Recently, I heard Tim Keller say in a podcast, "Our identity is received, not achieved." Christ alone is our identity, not our conquests or consequences. When Christ is your identity, you will experience refreshment and joy as you cling to your new inheritance as beloved, chosen son or daughter of the King of Kings.

If you are currently being inundated with hurtful names that are tearing you apart, I want to reassure you that God is *El Roi*, which means the God who sees. He sees everything. He promises to give you His strength to persevere under this trial and give you rest in the palms of His hands. Whatever you have done or said that brings a sense of failure or shame is covered by the grace of our Lord. Christ is more than sufficient to make up for whatever deficit you feel. The names that your enemies have given you will not remain; they will blow away like dust in the wind. This season will not last forever, for you are God's precious child, and He will fight for your honor.

Life Lessons Learned

The closer we draw to the Lord in surrender, the more He sanctifies our hearts and lives so we can better reflect His character. Surrendering to the Lord's will eventually becomes as normal as breathing. Jesus often chooses people for ministry that the religious communities might want to discard. He looks at our heart and wants to disentangle us from the hindrances that hold us back. This means we need to ask the Holy Spirit to cut away the lies we have been told and the false identities we have allowed to define us. Often there is a period of waiting on God before we can see His redemptive plan for our lives.

Waiting on God is one of the most spiritually challenging and mature decisions we can make. Trusting in God's timing and not our own will produce much fruit in our lives. Nothing is wasted in life, for all of our personal challenges and victories become etched into our cross stories. These cross stories are pointers to God's faithfulness, and He masterfully weaves them together into our unique calling. Part of living into our calling and identity as a child of the living God is to blot out the lies and believe God's promises instead. The "Wounded Identity vs. Redeemed Identity Chart," located in appendix 1, will walk you through the process of healing your wounded identity. It is important to be strong in your redeemed identity to ground you in Christ before you find yourself in a spiritual battle.

CLIMB THE MOUNTAIN
SCENE 3

Waiting on God can turn into a fierce spiritual battle for our heart's allegiance. While I hiked through a steep and rocky section of the trail, I reflected on my personal seasons of waiting and how my faith was tested. The long periods of silence chipped away at my resolve, causing my emotions to teeter on the precipice of doubt and despair. To be honest, there were times when I contemplated giving up, but I discerned that idea was a lie from the Enemy of my soul. The Lord kept prompting me to write for Him, so I persevered. Slowing down was against my nature, so I needed God's help to do so, and He answered my prayer in a way that I least expected.

My hiking boot got caught on a tree root, and my ankle rolled over. I felt a pop and then a shooting pain from the arch of my foot all the way up to my calf. "Fantastic!" I griped out loud in total frustration. *Now what?* I hobbled over to the closest rock and sat down to inspect the damage. I gingerly put my full weight on my foot to check the intensity of the injury. The sharp pain took my breath away. I prayed and pondered whether I should continue. Elephant's Head is an easy mountain to climb under normal circumstances, but my injury would make the journey much more challenging and longer. God had brought me on this hike for a reason, and I am familiar with pushing through pain. With grit and determination, the decision was made. I would *not* give up. It was settled. I would press on and continue to climb the mountain. As I limped along, I felt a flood of God's peace wash over my resolve.

With each step, my injury was a glaring reminder of my dependence on Christ. Sometimes we can let our woundedness get in the way of what God has for us, like the lesson He is trying to teach us or the blessing He wants to provide. The injury slowed down my

Our personal pain has a purpose, and suffering can serve as a tutor of wisdom.

pace, allowing me the time to fully appreciate the beauty in the Adirondack woods. I noticed intricate details of nature I might have missed if I had been walking at a faster clip. Resting allowed me the time to discover different kinds of birds, colorful mushrooms, and various shades of color in the fall leaves. The wilderness landscape was breathtakingly beautiful, with babbling brooks and moss-covered rocks. Streams of light pierced the forest's darkness like a sword, illuminating once-invisible snares.

As I looked closer, my heart skipped a beat, and I gasped! The light exposed an elaborate, hidden spider web that literally spanned the entire width of the trail. The intricacy of the web was beautiful in its design but deadly to its smaller prey. If I had been hiking faster, I would have undoubtedly ended up in the spider's snare. The horrifying scene from the movie *The Lord of the Rings: Return of the King*, when the gigantic spider tried to sedate and eat Frodo and Sam, came to mind. I shivered at the thought. My attitude changed to one of gratitude to be walking at a slower pace so I could avoid unexpected traps and snares. I used my trekking pole to clear the spider webs away with ease and continued on the trail set out before me.

At that moment, I was reminded that our personal pain has a purpose, and suffering can serve as a tutor of wisdom. Even though I was in pain with my injured foot, God continued to reveal meaningful metaphors paralleling life. The spider's web was not a threat to me, but the real Enemy's snare intends to kill, steal, and destroy. It was during the slower trek when I had the time to reflect on how to avoid the Enemy's traps and snares. As I move forward in faith, I'm grateful I can rely on Jesus to guide me up the mountain.

Scripture began to flood my thoughts, reminding me that I am never alone. "The Lord is my shepherd, I lack nothing. He makes me lie down in green pastures, he leads me beside quiet waters, he refreshes my soul. He guides me along the right paths for his name's sake. Even though I walk through the darkest valley, I will fear no evil, for you are with me" (Psalm 23:1–4 NIV). His faithful promise comforted me as I knew He would walk with me.

CHAPTER 3

BECOMING AWARE OF
THE ENEMY'S SNARE

But my eyes are fixed on you, Sovereign Lord; in you I take
refuge—do not give me over to death. Keep me safe from
the traps set by evildoers, from the snares they have laid for
me. Let the wicked fall into their own nets, while I pass by
in safety.

Psalm 141:8–10 NIV

Satan's Strategies

"The more powerful the testimony, the more forcefully he will try to destroy it. The devil wants to trip up a devoted follower of Christ."[1] This quote by Beth Moore reminds us that we need to be spiritually aware and on guard. Just like the light illuminated the giant spider webs on my hike, this chapter illuminates our real Enemy and his cunning snares that threaten to derail our calling. We must become aware of his tactics so we don't fall victim to his strategic traps. We'll spend time in chapter 4 learning about how to fight him using the tools and weapons God gives us to do battle effectively. For now, let's spend some time analyzing our real Enemy.

Ever since Lucifer (also called Satan) fell from heaven, he has worked overtime to accuse, kill, and destroy God's people. Isaiah 14:12–15 (NASB) tells the story of Lucifer's fall from the heavenly realm into the pit of hell because he said in his heart, "I will ascend to heaven;

I will raise my throne above the stars of God." I find it interesting that Satan first sinned in his heart with the prideful desire to rule above God. Proverbs 16:18 (NIV) says, "Pride goes before destruction, a haughty spirit before a fall." Pride was the root issue which caused Satan to fall from grace, a warning for you and me.

"Satan, who is a wonderful contriver of delusions, is constantly laying snares to entrap ignorant and heedless persons."[2] He has been given many titles and names in the Bible, which include the devil, Enemy, Father of Lies, Prince of this World, and Ruler of Demons, to name a few. Satan's character and methodology of destruction is to lie, murder, and deceive by twisting the truth. "Satan offers you what he cannot give; he is a liar and has been from the foundation of the world."[3] He hunts for opportunities to accuse, divide, and destroy relationships. He especially delights in terrorizing and targeting God's ambassadors who are faithfully seeking to evangelize and disciple Christ followers. Anyone in a position of spiritual influence or leadership is a focused target for Satan's attacks. "The Bible says that Satan's purpose is to blind sinners and beguile Christians, and to hurt and discourage those who belong to God. He will do anything to disturb the mind, deceive the heart, and defeat life."[4] Rest assured, you are not the only one under attack. Satan has bombarded godly men and women with his deceptive lies ever since the fall of mankind in the Garden of Eden.

This is how original sin in the garden happened. In Genesis 3:1–7 (NIV), Satan, in his craftiness, posed as a serpent in the garden and approached Eve to ask her a question in a way that would cause doubt in her mind: "Did God *really* say, 'You shall not eat from *any* tree in the garden'?"

Eve, attempting to correct Satan, said, "We may eat fruit from the trees in the garden, but God did say, you must not eat fruit from the tree that is in the middle of the garden, and you must not touch it or you will die."

Satan then twisted the truth and caused Eve to doubt by saying, "You will not certainly die," in what I imagine was a mocking tone. He tore down her confidence in her relationship with God by implying that she hadn't heard God correctly and that God was holding out on her for the best things in life. "Satan's goal is to deafen us to God's voice so that we embrace his thinking as easily and naturally as if it were God's very own."[5] Satan made Eve think that the death was a physical death, but God meant a spiritual death. Being cast out of God's presence is a fate much worse.

Satan persuasively argued again and said, "For God knows that when you eat from it your eyes will be opened, and you will be like God, knowing good and evil." The fruit was a delight to Eve's eyes, and she desired to become wise, so she ate of the tree and gave some to Adam (v.6). Eve was deceived in her mind and with her eyes, which led to her being deceived in her heart. Sin is always a slippery slope that can quickly derail us. "The devil never points out the abundant blessings of God in your life. The devil always points out what is missing, lacking or negative."[6] Refuse to listen to his lies.

What started out as a small twisting of truth, the seed of deception germinated into an insatiable longing, which resulted in Adam's and Eve's sin of eating the forbidden fruit. Adam was equally responsible because he heard the warning the Lord gave about not eating from the tree of the knowledge of good and evil, yet he ignored God's command. That catastrophic decision was the beginning of the end for mankind, launching all of us out of perfect fellowship with God in the garden and into Satan's realm for torment and destruction. "It is foolish to underestimate the power of Satan, but it is fatal to overestimate it."[7]

Even though the events of the fall took place long ago, Satan is as strategic today as he was in the garden. We must know his strategies so we don't fall into the same trap. Satan's approach was to twist God's words, distorting His motive to lure Adam and Eve into thinking God was withholding good things from them. Satan's seeds of doubt caused them to question God's character, His love, and His Word. Satan's lies planted a desire in Eve's heart to have something not meant for her—a forbidden fruit that she desired more than what God had already given her.

Let me ask you something. Is there a forbidden fruit that Satan is tempting you with today? "Satan wants your desires to master you, rather than you mastering your desires."[8] Be forewarned that forbidden fruit will never satisfy as it will turn into ashes in your mouth.

You see, Satan built lies on top of lies to convince Eve to doubt herself that she must not have heard God's words correctly. "The devil will use *our* words and *his* dictionary."[9] He twists the meaning and causes confusion. Out of Satan's persuasive words, unbelief entered Adam's and Eve's hearts, which led them both to sinful rebellion against God. "The devil works in many ways—sometimes openly, more often indirectly. But his goal is always the same: to turn us away from God."[10] After Adam and Eve ate of the tree they were forbidden to eat from, their innocence died when their eyes were opened, and they experienced shame, fear, and blame for the first time. The consequences of spiritual isolation were much greater than they ever could have imagined. All these negative emotions caused them to try to hide from God. This is still true today. Whenever we feel shame, guilt, fear, and other draining emotions, our fleshly nature wants to hide too. Satan wants us to be in isolation so we will be more vulnerable to his accusations and attacks.

Sin entered the human race in the garden, and a battle for souls has raged ever since. Adam's and Eve's choices have caused consequences for all humanity. Since the fall, sin has been continually passed down through the seed of Adam, and we are all born with a sinful nature, doomed to die separated from God. That is why we are in desperate need of a Savior. That is why we needed a new Adam, Jesus Christ, to cleanse us and give us a new nature that is not bound by sin. Adam brought sin into the world, but Jesus Christ, our Savior, provided a solution to the problem of sin through His death and resurrection.

Through Christ, our relationship with God is restored, and we are given the power of the Holy Spirit to break the control of sin in our lives. "Yes, Adam's one sin brings condemnation for everyone, but Christ's one act of righteousness brings a right relationship with God and a new life for everyone" (Romans 5:18 NLT). Praise God, we are no longer condemned! We are cleansed through the blood of Christ shed on the cross for you and for me. We owe our very lives to Jesus. It is the only appropriate response to follow Him wholeheartedly.

But even though we have been set free from sin's chains, Satan is constantly trying to convince us that we are not free. Satan wants us to believe we are still enslaved to our sin struggles which can rob us of hope for a better future. If hope is taken from us, then people lose the will to press on.

When I worked in the care ministry at my church in Chicago, I witnessed many Christians who loved the Lord but still felt chained to pornography, eating disorders, or alcohol addictions. There were divorced Christians who still felt shame over their failed marriages. Sadly, these believers were still enslaved in their minds, suffering under the burden of feeling like a failure as a Christian. I listened to people's stories entailing extramarital affairs or abortions, and they still did not feel forgiven or set free even after authentic repentance and remorse. Our faith in Christ must supersede our feelings. "Satan is a liar, deceiver, and a counterfeiter. And it is important for all of us to know that he is real and that he is doing everything he can to make our walk with Jesus and our witness for Him ineffective."[11] Satan is masterful at trying to beat down and immobilize Christians so we remain stuck and defeated.

But even though we have been set free from sin's chains, Satan is constantly trying to convince us that we are not free. Satan wants us to believe we are still enslaved to our sin struggles, which can rob us of hope for a better future.

But the blood of Christ shed on the cross was sufficient to cover all of our sins and sever the power of sin and death. We have been forgiven and set free for a higher calling. A Christ-follower who has been set free from bondage is one of the greatest witnesses of Christ's transformative power. People around us are eager to hear how the change in us happened. But Satan wants to silence us so we don't proclaim the freedom that is available with Jesus. So, shake off the lies and start embracing a bold, unquenchable faith.

Father of Lies

The Father of Lies loses his power over us when we stop giving emotional weight and mental assent to his lies. For us to live freely, it is imperative to understand the strategies and character of our real Enemy. Identifying the true source of the lie helps us to negate the message of the liar. Satan's strategy is to constantly spread lies to slander God's people and to create confusion about God's character. John 8:44 (NLT) says, "He was a murderer from the beginning. He has always hated the truth, because there is no truth in him. When he lies, it is consistent with his character; for he is a liar and the father of lies."

Satan spins his lies into a huge web of deception and then uses people to perpetuate his lies. That is why the tongue is so critically important to control. Our words can be used to build up others in the body of Christ or tear each other down and defile an entire community. "So also, the tongue is a small member, yet it boasts of great things. How great a forest is set ablaze by such a small fire!" (James 3:5 ESV). One lie can spark a red-hot blazing fire that can destroy someone's entire reputation and honor within a matter of minutes. The power of a lie can cause fierce destruction, and that is why it is critical to be careful with our words, theories, and assumptions. Even factual information needs to be prayed over before it is shared with others. Ask yourself, is sharing this information edifying the body of Christ?

I know this kind of personal attack all too well. When you are on the frontlines doing God's kingdom work, there will be both opportunities and opposition. A forest fire of lies kept me isolated and alone for way too many years. The confusion and grief over being misrepresented, shunned, and treated horribly was almost more than I could handle. It is only by the grace of God that I survived, and He is the one who has helped me to persevere in the power of the Holy Spirit. I will be forever grateful to Him for sustaining me.

Satan first deceives people in their minds, then uses their lips to perpetuate the spread of gossip, solidifying the lie in their hearts as a false sense of truth. "When it comes to lying, deceiving, and twisting the truth, the devil is truly in a class all his own. He's a liar by nature, and his entire motivation—his reason for being—is to lie and deceiove."[12]

Repetition is part of Satan's brainwashing strategy. People falsely believe that if you have heard information repeatedly, then it must be true. Unfortunately, the internet and social media have created a virtual playground for Satan's lies to be spread around the world with great speed, causing mass destruction. Think about it. With the click of a button, damaging words can be posted on Facebook, Twitter, or Instagram. There is no undo button in cyberspace. It is a growing, tragic epidemic in which people are committing suicide because of being cyberbullied, identity hacked, or slandered over social media. This is heartbreaking!

"Satan is not mainly interested in causing us misery. He is mainly interested in making Christ look bad. He hates Christ. And he hates the glory of Christ. He will do all he can to keep people from seeing Christ as glorious."[13] As Christians, it is imperative for us to hold our tongues captive and to speak only what is edifying, encouraging, and full of God's love and truth. This kind of speech brings glory to God.

Condemnation vs. Conviction

Are you eager to experience the thrilling adventure of the mountaintop, or do you want to remain stuck at the bottom of the valley? Discerning the difference between condemnation and conviction will determine the outcome of your trekking adventure. The choice is between living enslaved or living free. The internal and external bombardment and burden of Satan's lies can weigh us down like an overloaded, heavy backpack. We can subconsciously fall into internal condemnation if we replay in our minds all of the horrible falsehoods and cruel experiences.

Remember, "Satan is the master of accusation."[14] In an exhausted, overwhelmed, or vulnerable state of mind, the weight of condemnation can leave us feeling emotionally beat up and completely drained.

If we feel as though we have failed God, failed someone we love, or failed ourselves, it is a slippery slope down into the insidious pit of self-condemnation. It is similar to trailblazing through the woods, when all of a sudden, you step into a hole of quicksand; every time you move, the sand pulls you deeper into a downward spiral. My friend, you need Christ-centered help! It is virtually impossible to get out of the pit on your own strength or willpower. If you try to get free on your own, you will sink deeper into the sand trap.

One of the key verses that helped me survive the pit of shame and condemnation from feeling branded "divorced" was Romans 8:1 (NASB), "Therefore there is now no condemnation for those who are in Christ Jesus." I repeated that Scripture so many times to remind myself that the Lord loves me as His precious child. Thankfully, God doesn't label me "divorced." He knows my heart and the complete story. I honored the covenant of my marriage and was faithful to my ex-husband throughout our marriage and separation. I even wore my wedding band for the entire eighteen months until the divorce was finalized.

Since I've been single again, I have remained consistent with my devotion to Christ. The Holy Spirit dwells within me, and I want to honor God with my body and my life. If I am ever blessed with a second chance at a Christ-centered marriage, it will be incredibly healing and redemptive, I'm sure. In the meantime, I am content with my singleness, which allows me to be totally focused on God's mission and calling. I've been blessed beyond measure by stronger relationships with my family and friends. It has been a dream come true to have the time to write about God's faithfulness and how to follow His leading.

How does one understand the difference between condemnation and conviction? Many people get tripped up by this, so let's think about it. First off, it begins with whose voice you are listening to—God's or

Satan's. You can tell whose voice you are listening to by the *fruit* that is produced in your life.

Condemnation is a favorite tool Satan uses to discourage, oppress, and bring despair during our vulnerable seasons. Condemnation is from the voice of Satan, which produces the bad fruit of hopelessness, bitterness, chaos, confusion, anger, and despair. Condemnation from Satan is often based on shame, guilt, or fear, and it is life-taking.

By contrast, conviction comes from the Lord. Conviction is life-giving because ultimately it is life changing. Through conviction by the Holy Spirit, God illuminates truth and exposes the dark areas in our lives. Conviction creates the desire to die to our sinful nature and embrace our new nature, who we are in Christ. When the Holy Spirit convicts us of our sin, He produces what I call an ouch-hallelujah-thank-you-Jesus moment. *Ouch*, the confrontation of our sin hurts, but *hallelujah*, it leads us to confession, repentance, and *thank you Jesus*, because it ultimately brings about new life. Be warned, though, Satan's attacks of condemnation can be relentless, accusing and penetrating our thoughts even after we've repented and asked God for forgiveness. When this happens, you can know it comes from Satan, for God says, "As far as the eastern horizon is from the west, so he removes the guilt of our rebellious actions from us" (Psalm 103:12 NET). Once we have confessed and repented of our mistakes, God remembers them no more, so why would He continue to bring it up? He wouldn't.

The difference between condemnation and conviction is as clear as swimming in a fresh mountain lake versus trying to swim in a weed-entrenched bog. While visiting The Wild Center Museum in Tupper Lake, New York, I learned while reading the plaque above the display that the bog plant (sphagnum) "manipulates its surroundings to wipe out its competition"[15] to create a space for it to thrive and grow. The bog plant destroys other lifeforms by consuming all the water, removing the nutrients from the healthy water, and literally "spits back an acid bath"[16] into the bog. Sphagnum buries other plants as it grows at a higher elevation, blocking out the sunlight, which cools down the

ARISE, AND CLIMB THE MOUNTAIN

temperature of the water causing other plant life, fish, and even trees to die. It basically takes over the entire pond by killing all life forms.

That is what condemnation does to us—it spreads like cancer and consumes us to the point where we feel dead inside. But we have Christ, who convicts and disciplines because He loves us (Proverbs 3:12). "Being confronted on character issues isn't pleasant. It hurts our self-image. It humbles us. But it doesn't harm us. Loving confrontation protects us from blindness and self-destructiveness."[17] When we turn to the Lord in repentance, He makes us a new creation.

Invisible Traps

One day, as I walked down the front porch steps and followed the stone path to the dock for my daily quiet time with the Lord, I noticed a blueberry bush loaded with ripe berries. At that moment, the sun came up over the mountains, and my eyes caught a glimpse of a perfectly symmetrical spider web hovering on the outer branches of the blueberry bush. The web was approximately two feet high and wide, and there was not a single tear in it. *Whoa, that cunning little spider's web is strategically placed,* I thought—much like the web across the trail. The web was invisible to me until the morning sunlight exposed the web's sticky threads.

I know it is part of God's ecosystem design for spiders to eat flies for food, but I still wanted to protect the underdog, or "underfly" in this case. Out of compassion, I placed several small leaves on the invisible web to warn the flies of their impending doom if they decided to land on the blueberry bush. I later noticed that my effort to warn the flies was futile as the spider removed my carefully placed leaves from its sticky spindles. I recalled a previous time when I saw a fly much bigger than the size of the spider get caught in the web. The poor, unsuspecting fly couldn't break free from the sticky entrapment, and it finally exhausted itself and gave up. The spider often waits for the fly to be at its most vulnerable point of exhaustion before it moves in for the kill.

I know what it feels like to be tangled up in a web of deception, sedated by venomous lies, and virtually immobilized. The predicament of the fly is parallel to being a prisoner of the invisible stronghold of Satan's lies that he has tightly spun around you to bind you from living the life of freedom and joy the Lord has designed for you.

After seven years of enjoying God's favor with a thriving ministry, I began to have a growing sense of holy discontentment. I knew in my heart that God was preparing me to move to another ministry calling; I just didn't know when, where, or what. I vividly remember praying a dangerous Isaiah 6:8 prayer for God to "send me" and use me where I was most needed. I thought He would send me to another church or a Christian nonprofit, but I had absolutely no idea I would be moving back to Connecticut to help my family navigate through several challenging crises. After twenty years of living in the Midwest, the East Coast was the last place I expected to be sent.

Being a visible Christian leader in ministry is a great privilege, but it also makes you a target for the Enemy to attack and try to discredit your witness. Sadly, erroneous speculations surrounded my choice to resign from my ministry position. The truth is, I prayed about it for many months before I took action. I am grateful that God produced much fruit in the ministry over the years and He was glorified through it. My pastor was utterly shocked at the announcement that I was resigning from my ministry position because he knew the depth of my dedication to furthering the kingdom of God in Chicago. We still need to follow Jesus out of loving obedience even when it doesn't make sense.

Like Abraham, though, God was asking me to pick up and leave my home for a destination unknown. I followed His lead because I trust Him with my life, and my heart's desire is to serve Him. I stepped out in faith, but I was shocked when everything radically changed; it felt as though I had stepped on a land mine. Everything I had worked so hard for, over many years, was suddenly blown up into a million pieces. There was no moral failure or crisis of faith. I just stepped out in faith to follow the Holy Spirit's leading.

The Lord mercifully reassured me after I read in the *Streams in the Desert* devotional, "After blessings comes the battle. The time of testing that distinguishes and greatly enriches a person's spiritual career is not an ordinary one but a period when it seems as if all hell were set loose. It is a time when we realize that our soul is caught in a net, and we know God is allowing us to be gripped by the devil's hand. Yet it is a period that always ends in a certain triumph for those who have committed the keeping of their souls to God. And the testing 'later on . . . produces a harvest of righteousness and peace' (Hebrews 12:11) and paves the way for the thirtyfold to one hundredfold increase that is promised to follow (see Matthew 13:23)."[18] The hope that I gleaned from the devotional message helped me to press on in faith during this confusing season. I needed this anchor for my soul, because every time I turned around, I was bombarded with another lie.

Words are like weapons that can cut deep into your soul, so I shielded myself by driving to our camp in the Adirondacks. Spending time writing at our camp at Lake Titus was the perfect place for healing. Writing about God's faithfulness helped protect me from hopelessness. While I was sitting in the Adirondack chair, I prayed that God would use my pain for His glory. Somehow, someway. Our compassionate Lord inspired me to start writing a book to bring hope to the brokenhearted.

If you are struggling with feeling immobilized, I want to reassure you: God's got this. The Lord is greater than your circumstance. In an instant, He can effortlessly tear down this complex web of lies that has imprisoned you. God can and will destroy Satan's web with a swish of His mighty finger. In His perfect timing, He will rescue you.

Our personal mountains may still loom large in front of us, but God promises to light our path one step at a time. Psalm 119:105 (NIV) says, "Your word is a lamp for my feet, a light on my path." With Christ, we can persevere through our struggles and have faith in His sovereign plan for us. "You can rest in the knowledge that even when bad things happen, God is always there. He is always in charge. Although He may not always deliver you in the way that you expect, you will find his grace sufficient."[19] I'm grateful that we can look forward to the future when the Lord will produce a great harvest of righteousness using our wilderness experiences.

Stone Lions

The Holy Spirit helps us see our real Enemy is not flesh and blood but rather the deceiver. Second Corinthians 11:14 (ESV) informs us that "Satan goes around disguising himself as an angel of light" in order to deceive God's people and lead them astray. We are warned to "beware of false prophets, who come to you in sheep's clothing but inwardly are ravenous wolves" (Matthew 7:15 ESV). That is why Scripture tells us to be wise as serpents and as gentle as doves. Elizabeth George wisely stated to "make no decision without prayer."[20] The Lord promises to guide us with His wisdom and discernment when we pray about everything—every opportunity, every situation, and every relationship.

While walking down Clark Street in the historic Swedish neighborhood in Chicago, I passed by my favorite Middle Eastern restaurant, Reza's. The outdoor portion of the restaurant has a charming ambiance with bistro tables and spring flowers overflowing from the baskets alongside the fence. After my eyes took in the beautiful scene, I became fixed on a three-foot-tall stone lion. The Scripture passage came to mind from 1 Peter 5:8 (ESV): "Be sober-minded; be watchful. Your adversary the devil prowls around like a roaring lion, seeking someone to devour."

God often speaks to me in metaphors, and it was almost like an audible voice saying, *Sharon, Satan is like that stone lion. He looks just like a fierce lion complete with fangs and claws, but he can't hurt you. I won't let him hurt you because Satan is still under my authority.* How often, I wondered, do we look at fierce lions in our lives and live with fear and anxiety over the harm they could potentially cause us? Satan will try to hurt us physically and emotionally, but he will never be able to take our souls because we belong to Christ. The truth is this: nothing touches us that does not first pass through God's loving fingers for a purpose. God is still in control even when we are in the pit facing lions.

I think we give Satan too much power over our lives through the stronghold of fear. The Scriptures tell us not to fear your enemies, only have a reverential fear of the Lord. Mary Southerland says it this way, "Confidence in God's presence is our basic weapon against fear."[21] When we experience the power of an intense storm roaring across the lake or see the multitude of stars in the heavens on a clear night or witness the bond between a newborn fawn with its mother, we see glimpses of the greatness of God. When we have reverential fear of the Lord, we acknowledge that He reigns over the heavens and the earth. This creates a heart of worship for the majesty of God.

The Holy Spirit gives us His power and wisdom to combat fear of Satan. "Fear can be conquered only by faith, and faith thrives on truth."[22] Truth is found in God's Word. Is Satan fierce, vile, deceptive, cruel, and cunning? Absolutely! But Satan is *not* on equal par with God. God's authority reigns supreme *over* Satan. Pastor Jay Abramson had fresh insights into what it really means to be afraid of Satan. He said, "Fearing Satan is the same as worshiping him, and Satan accepts your fear as worship. The truth is Satan is a dead man walking. When Satan reminds you of your past sins and failures, you should remind him of his future."[23] Part of Satan's strategy is to deceive you into thinking that he is to be feared more than God.

Another lie is that God either doesn't care about your pain or is powerless to stop the suffering. Both are untrue. God declares, "For as the heavens are higher than the earth, so are my ways higher than your ways and my thoughts than your thoughts" (Isaiah 55:9 NIV). If God permits evil to touch us, it is for a higher purpose beyond our comprehension.

Satan and his demons are limited in their ability, power, and knowledge. Satan cannot be in all places at the same time; only God can. Dr. David Jeremiah said, "For all his power, Satan is neither omnipotent, omniscient, nor omnipresent. His power has limitations, and he can only act within the limits imposed upon him by God. God is greater than Satan and his evil, which will never be able to separate Christians from God's love."[24] Some demons are free to roam the earth like a roaring lion looking for someone to devour, and some are in chains in darkness (1 Peter 5:8; Jude 1:6 NIV).

Satan and his demons cannot read our minds, for only God knows our thoughts. However, they watch us closely and observe our behaviors, words, and how we react to circumstances. They look for ways to tempt us, twist our words, and distort the truth. "The Enemy of our souls knows where our flesh is the weakest and he will put temptations in our path at our most vulnerable points."[25] Satan is a student of our vulnerabilities, and he searches for an opportunity to pounce on our character, destroy our witness, and squelch our faith in Christ.

God Reigns

Our spiritual battles are not between two equal forces, God versus Satan. Nor is the battle fought on an equal playing field. God created the field, He owns the field, and He knows everything about every single player. Our Sovereign God rules over heaven and earth, and everyone and everything must bow to His supreme authority. Satan would like us to believe the lie that he is stronger when we are being railed against. Not true! Satan will *never* be equal to God's supreme authority. God reigns over all!

One of Satan's favorite lies is that God doesn't care about us enough to rescue us from our struggles. That is a lie from the pit of hell! The truth in His Word says, "Cast all your anxiety on him because he cares for you" (1 Peter 5:7 NIV). God loves us, He cares for us, and He alone holds the power to change situations. The Lord loved and cared for us so much that He was willing to die for us. There is no greater love.

Time of Testing

"Before God can truly use us, in one way or another, we will pass through a time of threshing."[26] Job's life is an example of being threshed like wheat. In the Old Testament, Satan had to ask God's permission to test Job's faith by inflicting fierce adversity and hardship on him (Job 1:12). God knew Job's faithful heart, so He allowed Satan to test Him—with a boundary that Job's life must be spared. When the test of faith was finished, and Job still worshiped God, God restored his fortunes and blessed him with double the amount than he had before. "God's blessings are dispersed according to the riches of his grace, not according to the depth of our faith."[27]

A New Testament passage in Luke demonstrates God's supreme power and authority. After Jesus told Peter that he would deny Him, Jesus said, "Simon, Simon, behold, Satan has asked to sift all of you like wheat" (Luke 22:31 NIV). Satan tested the disciples and hoped to tear their faith apart when their Savior died on the cross and their world was turned upside down. Satan's plans failed, and the disciples became stronger through their time of testing. "Just as God allowed Job, John the Baptist, and many other faithful believers to be tested and troubled beyond their human strength, He may test us."[28] A time of testing can certainly bring anguish, but the Lord can use our sorrow as a refining instrument to grow and mature our faith.

Life Lessons Learned

Our pain can be used for a divine purpose. Being forced to hike at a slower pace allowed me to see things from God's perspective so I could avoid the hidden snares on the trail, as well as in life. This chapter illuminated some of Satan's strategies and his uses of fear, condemnation, lies, and deception to throw us off God's path. "Because Satan's primary weapon is the lie, your defense against him is the truth. Dealing with Satan is not a power encounter; it is a truth encounter."[29] It doesn't matter how many years you have been in bondage to Satan's lies, God's truth in His Word can tear apart the web of lies that surrounds you.

When we work together as a united team, instead of fighting each other, God is glorified, and Satan's plans are defeated.

Our real enemies are not the people we can see; rather, the real Enemy is in the spiritual realm. In *The Strategy of Satan*, Warren Wiersbe says, "Satan and his hosts are organized. If only believers could be united in their defense and their warfare, Satan would not win so many victories. Sad to say, Christians too often are so busy fighting one another that they have no time for fighting the devil."[30] When we work together as a united team, instead of fighting each other, God is glorified, and Satan's plans are defeated.

Friend, this information about Satan's strategies is not to make you afraid, but to make you wary and wise about the spiritual warfare we find ourselves in every single day. As we humble ourselves and listen to the Lord's voice, He will give us wisdom to see Satan's strategies and discern his lies.

Spiritual warfare and opposition should not be a surprise to us, because they were foretold in the Scriptures long ago. Daniel 7:25 (NASB) tells us the Enemy "will speak against the Most High and wear down the saints of the Highest One." Satan is trying to wear out the people of God and exhaust them by tearing down their witness and effectiveness for Christ. Do not fear, because the Lord has given us His spiritual armor and plenty of spiritual gear, strategies, and tactics to fight him victoriously, which we'll get into in the next chapter.

Remember, Christ has already won the battle at the cross. We are on the winning side!

CLIMB THE MOUNTAIN
SCENE 4

My thoughts drifted as I was captivated with the beauty of a delicate wildflower in the woods. Caught unaware, I had a rather rude awakening of searing pain when my already injured and swollen foot stubbed a rock in the middle of the path. I gasped out loud and limped over to a fallen log where I could rest for a while. *This was supposed to be an easy, short hike*, I grumbled. Questions of doubt and accusations flooded into my mind. *What if my foot gets so swollen I can't walk anymore? Will I get stuck on the mountain overnight?* I wished I had brought a cell phone, a headlamp, or a thermo-blanket. *What was I thinking?* Bent over in defeat, I let out another heavy sigh, which turned into a loud groan. I wanted to give up on my quest to climb the mountain.

Mercifully, the Lord interrupted my self-deprecating thoughts and reassured me this was all part of His bigger plan. He reminded me of all the spiritual gear I had been given through the Holy Spirit. My perspective began to change as I rehearsed God's promises in His Word. The Lord promised to be my strength when I am weak. He promised to walk with me through the valley and take me to the mountaintop. He promised to be my protector and provider. The Lord reassured me that I am not alone on this mountain, for He is with me still and always.

When I leaned back and looked up toward the light shining through the trees, I remembered my gear in my backpack. I had an Ace bandage for support, Advil to bring down the swelling, and water to hydrate. My trekking poles took the pressure off my foot and steadied my balance. I didn't have everything I wanted, but God provided all the hiking equipment and spiritual gear I needed to climb the mountain before me. With each step, my awareness increased as I reflected how our spiritual battles are often a triple attack on our mind, body, and emotions. Thankfully, through the Holy Spirit, I have been given the armor of God and spiritual tactics to overcome the Enemy's plans.

CHAPTER 4

WINNING THE SPIRITUAL BATTLE

Be strong in the Lord and in his mighty power. Put on all of God's armor so that you will be able to stand firm against all strategies of the devil.

Ephesians 6:10–11 NLT

Spiritual Perspective

Our invisible Enemy may have a battle plan for our demise, but we are *not* spiritually defenseless. By faith, we have been equipped with several weapons of protection for our mind, body, and emotions. It is imperative to learn how to utilize the equipment *before* we need it. Think about it. Imagine being in the thick of a personal crisis or spiritual battle and completely forgetting how to protect ourselves. I am certain the outcome would not be pretty. This chapter will demonstrate how the Holy Spirit has equipped us with His spiritual gear to be triumphant over our spiritual battles and off-trail trekking.

Most importantly, before we hit the trail, we need to remind ourselves that no matter what happens, God is still sovereign. Simply put, God is in control and we are not. This world is filled with personal mountains to climb, and if we desire to be successful mountain climbers, it begins with having a firm footing in faith. Unfortunately, I needed to learn this lesson the hard way.

Several weeks after arriving at Lake Titus, I spontaneously decided to take my kayak over to the protected forest inlets on the southwest end of the lake. The wildlife is drawn to the undisturbed waters in this undeveloped wooded area to build their nests and raise their young. In the past, I have seen bald eagles, blue herons, kingfisher birds, freshwater otters, merganser ducks, loons, and beavers in the "forever wild" inlets. The lake was like glass without a single boat to disturb the still waters. As I glided to my destination, I heard the rushing sound of water and instantly remembered the hidden mountain stream in the forest. I paddled over to the area and pulled my kayak onto the shoreline.

I hate to admit I was unprepared for an Adirondack hiking adventure that morning as I had worn flip-flops instead of hiking boots. I was painfully aware of my bad choice as I disastrously attempted to bushwhack through the dense forest over slippery rocks, roots, fallen trees, and muddy patches to get a better view of the mountain stream. My flip-flops malfunctioned several times, and I almost sprained my ankle when it rolled over. I was relieved that no one could see me stumbling through the forest. I laughed and thought, *I am a complete comedy of errors.*

Just then I took a giant step over the moss-covered rock, and my right foot sunk deep into the mud when my weight shifted. When the mud slid over my foot and part way up my ankle, I thought, *Oh no! How am I going to get out of here?* I struggled to extract my leg out of the thick mud, until finally, it released with a great suction sound, and I fell backward on the ground. My foot was free, but my favorite flip-flop will be forever buried in a muddy grave. I laughed out loud as I looked at my feet covered in mud with only one flip-flop. At this point, I realized my adventure was over and decided to gingerly hobble back on bare feet to the kayak.

As I paddled away, a spiritual analogy filled my thoughts. For us to experience the life adventure God designed for us long ago, our feet need to be standing on firm ground—on the truth of God's Word. Additionally, without a firm footing of faith, we will be ill-equipped to protect ourselves. A smaller animal stuck in the mud would be an easy target for a larger predator. The same is true for you and me. If we remain emotionally stuck in the mud of our painful circumstances, we will be an easy target for a spiritual attack. When we stand on the foundation of God's Word, however, we will be strong and ready, prepared for whatever comes our way.

For us to experience the life adventure God designed for us long ago, our feet need to be standing on firm ground— on the truth of God's Word.

As believers, we have a long history of being overcomers for the glory of God. Many spiritual battles have been fought and won in both the Old and New Testaments. These victory stories in the Bible grow our faith and reassure us that we can be overcomers too. In 2 Chronicles 20:1–30, the Lord took an impossible situation and made it possible for Judah to witness a miraculous victory. Three armies had joined forces to wage war against Judah. The people of Judah were clearly outnumbered, and their situation was dire. King Jehoshaphat mobilized an entire community to use their spiritual tactics, such as fasting, standing firm against their enemy, worshiping God, showing gratitude, giving God the glory in advance for their victory, and drawing strength from one another. Against all odds, God fought on their behalf and gave them victory over their enemies.

In the New Testament, the apostle Paul wrote Ephesians 6:10–20 under the divine inspiration of the Holy Spirit on how to put on the whole armor of God for protection. He used the analogy of spiritual weaponry, the gear God has given believers, comparing it to a Roman suit of armor. He described the helmet of salvation, the breastplate of righteousness, and the sword of the Spirit, God's Word. Paul dealt with the harsh reality of spiritual warfare on a regular basis, so he knew what he was talking about. While Paul was sharing the gospel, he endured being whipped five times with thirty-nine lashes, beaten three times with rods, stoned, shipwrecked, and bitten by a snake. He knew the ache of being hungry and thirsty, and yet He still survived with minimal provisions (2 Corinthians 11:23–26). Paul lived and breathed opposition daily, therefore we should not be surprised when we find ourselves in spiritual battles too.

"To go into battle without the 'full armor of God' is as foolish as a soldier entering the front lines dressed for a game of tennis."[1] As believers, we need to be prepared and equipped for our spiritual battles. We

What God says about us in His Word is greater than ten thousand lies from your worst enemy.

already discussed in chapter 3 that our real Enemy is from the unseen world of darkness governed by Satan and his followers, not the difficult people we interact with face to face. Seeing our earthly enemies through spiritual eyes can be a real perspective check for you and me. Remember, "A man's word is a little sound, that flies in the air, and soon vanishes; but the Word of God is greater than heaven and earth."[2] What God says about us in His Word is greater than ten thousand lies from your worst enemy.

Over the years, the Lord has refined me through many spiritual battles, and while God has healed my wounds, I still bear the scars. Redirecting my thought life has been profoundly helpful; instead of focusing on myself, I give praise to my healer for the many ways He has brought healing and redemption from unbearable situations. The Lord's perspective allows me to view my healed wounds as victory scars that symbolize being an overcomer.

"A proper perspective on spiritual warfare is focused on the power of God, rather than on the ploys of Satan."[3] We can be courageous warriors instead of timid people when facing a spiritual battle, using our spiritual gear and deploying spiritual tactics and strategies. Let's look at how to put on the armor of God and utilize our spiritual gear in the heat of a battle first, and then we'll delve into spiritual tactics we can use to gain strength and defeat the Enemy. You can refer to the chart in the appendix 2, "Victory Strategies: Spiritual Tactics, Gear & Weapons," which is helpful in summarizing all the different ways to do battle against the Enemy.

Spiritual Gear (Armor of God—Ephesians 6:10–20)

Belt of Truth

The belt of truth is one of the most powerful weapons against the master deceiver. When Satan lies to us, we can respond by reciting what is true based on Scripture. Even Jesus did this when He was tempted in the wilderness. God's Word reminds us what is true when false accusations rail against us. The belt of truth will also correct the lies we tell ourselves. Sometimes we are our own worst enemy in the way we tear ourselves down.

Breastplate of Righteousness

When Satan attacks our heart, emotions, and self-worth, we can speak out loud that we stand in the righteousness of Christ and not our own. Christ's breastplate will protect our hearts from the attack and remind us we are worthy and loved because of what Jesus did for us on the cross. He has taken our sin and given us His righteousness in its place. We are the children of God who have been cleansed of all our unrighteousness through Christ's sacrifice, and we have been made right with God.

Shoes of Peace

During a season of turmoil and confusion, we can stand firm on the solid rock and put on the shoes of peace. If we remain focused on Jesus, we will not slide down the mountain into the valley of chaos below. The hiking boots of peace will enable us to climb the mountain while sharing the peace of Christ with others. The Lord has given us His peace to live in harmony with each other and to rise above relational conflict. As believers, the peace of Christ that rules in our hearts allows us to be salt and light to a broken world. Keep trusting the Lord and sharing your testimony with others.

Shield of Faith

When Satan shoots his arrows filled with temptation, doubt, and fear, we can put up our shield of faith for protection. The Lord Almighty will cover us with a hedge of protection so we can keep fighting the good fight of faith and press on with perseverance. Our shield of faith protects us against an attack of despair by reminding us that the best is yet to come.

Helmet of Salvation

We are prepared for battle when Satan questions our salvation, baptism, or relationship with Jesus. Putting on the helmet of salvation allows us to say with godly confidence, we are saved by the blood of Jesus. Our salvation is secure because of Christ, and our names are written in the Lamb's Book of Life. We have been given God's blessed assurance of our salvation, and that cannot be taken from us. We are sealed by the Holy Spirit.

Sword of the Spirit

The Word of God cuts through every lie, but it also brings clarity, conviction, and healing. God's Word is living water to our souls because it reveals God's heart, character, and His glorious promises. The more we meditate and memorize the Word of God, the better equipped we will be to wield our sword. We can fight on the offensive with the sword of God's Word instead of struggling under condemnation and self-doubt. The sword of God's Word reminds us to focus on what is true, noble, right, pure, and lovely (Philippians 4:8).

Spiritual Tactics and Strategies (Ephesians 6 and 2 Chronicles 20)

There are a few additional tactics and strategies we can employ individually and together as a Christian community when faced with spiritual opposition. "God did not build the church for our safety but to equip us to win at spiritual warfare."[4] It is imperative that we stand on the truth that Christ has already won the war. We fight from victory. This next section is a combination of what Paul instructs us to do in Ephesians 6 and Jehoshaphat's successful battle plan in 2 Chronicles 20.

Stand Firm

We recognize that we are powerless in our own strength, but the Lord is all powerful and He promises to fight our battles. God repeatedly tells us to not be afraid or discouraged. The battle is the Lord's, and we can be confident that He will bring about a miraculous outcome. When we stand firm as a Christian community, we are stronger together than apart. There is strength in solidarity. Our job is to show up to the battle, put on our armor of God, and stand firm in our faith, believing God is fighting for us.

Fasting

Fasting is a powerful way to humble ourselves and seek the Lord's face for wisdom. God is faithful to guide us when we come to Him for direction. During our time of fasting and prayer, we can thank God for His faithfulness in the past and His character that never changes. It is a powerful strategy to pray back God's promises to remind us of God's love. This time of fasting allows us to hear the Lord more clearly when we seek Him for wisdom and direction.

Prayer

It is important to humble ourselves, repent of our sins, and thank God for His faithfulness before we ask for anything. It is essential to come to the Lord in prayer with believing faith, not halfhearted unbelief. We need to be spiritually alert and continuously praying for all ambassadors of Christ. Through intercessory prayer, the Lord will give us His wisdom, discernment, and protection right when we need it most. Remember, there is power and divine intervention when we cry out in Jesus's name!

Worshiping

We worship a miracle-working God, and He delights in overturning the plans of the Enemy. Just as Jehoshaphat praised the Lord in advance of the battle, so can we. It is a powerful spiritual weapon to praise and thank the Lord. The battle is the Lord's, and He will fight on our behalf while we worship Him. Worship will strengthen our spiritual resolve to trust in the only One who can save us.

Showing Gratitude

Jehoshaphat and his people immediately went to the temple and praised God with grateful hearts for the victorious outcome. The Lord blessed them with peace on every side. When we experience victory over our present-day battles, it is important to immediately thank God for His faithfulness and mercy. Our gratitude is a sweet fragrance to our heavenly Father.

Doing Battle with God's Word

The Christian life is not a cakewalk; it is a battlefield. "The problem is that so often we forget that we are in warfare and that Satan's target is our mind."[5] He plays mind games when we are most vulnerable. Early one morning, I was walking up the hill on the mile-long dirt road from our Lake Titus camp, and out of nowhere I was bombarded with memories of all my failures and inadequacies. I knew it was a spiritual battle, one I struggled against emotionally, as the onslaught of lies deceived me that I was not worthy to reach people for Christ, I was not good enough to write books or serve in ministry, and I would certainly never be used by God. Fortunately, God intervened by reminding me of the armor of God and how to apply my spiritual gear. "The sword of the Spirit, which is the Word of God is far more powerful than our own arguments."[6] God's Word always trumps our own words.

I remember shouting out loud, "Jesus who lives inside of me is greater than Satan who lives in this broken world," from (1 John 4:4, paraphrase mine). Immediately after speaking Scripture out loud, I felt lighter, like a heavy weight on my shoulders had been released. God's peace filled my mind, and I continued to fight the lies with the sword of God's Word, proclaiming His promise for survival, "When you pass through the rivers, they will not sweep over you. When you walk through the fire, you will not be burned; the flames will not set you ablaze" (Isaiah 43:2 NIV). I repeated the Scripture over and over again until I was strengthened, empowered, and liberated by His divine reassurance.

God's promises are packed with healing truth and freedom. "The mere reading of the Word of God has the power to communicate the life of God to us mentally, morally and spiritually."[7] Proclaiming God's Word out loud has the power to defuse the intensity of the accusations and lies. Even Jesus used the Scriptures to fight Satan's lies in the wilderness when He was being tempted. "If the Son of God felt it necessary to respond to Satan's specific lies with God's specific truths, what does that say about us?"[8] How much more should we use the sword of God's Word to fend off the Enemy?

Calling on the Powerful Name of Jesus

Another powerful strategy we can use is the very name of Jesus. I have experienced firsthand its indescribable power. Jesus's authority as Son of God and Son of Man can bring the dead back to life, calm the storms, and heal the blind. Scripture says, "Therefore God has highly exalted him and bestowed on him the name that is above every name, so that at the name of Jesus every knee should bow, in heaven and on earth and under the earth" (Philippians 2:9–10 ESV). The disciples healed the sick and the lame, cast out demons, and performed amazing miracles, all with the power and authority of Jesus's name. It wasn't the disciples' power that healed but Christ working through them. As followers of Christ, we can call on His name to rescue us from dangerous situations.

The heavy snow had been coming down for hours before the high winds started blowing the snow sideways across the highway. I silently wondered if it was worth the risk driving to Vermont in this blizzard for our ski trip. The temperature gauge lowered well below the freezing mark, which concerned me because of the potential for creating black ice on the road. My friend driving the car thrived on stressful driving challenges. He was speeding faster than was comfortable to me, so I gripped the side of the car for dear life. Suddenly, we hit a patch of black ice while turning on a steep curve. The black ice spun our car at full speed toward the mountain cliff overlooking the valley below.

I gasped out of sheer fright. I was not ready for a Thelma-and-Louise-flying-off-the-cliff-in-their-car experience, so I prayed at the top of my lungs, *"Jesus, help us!"* In an instant, the car rotated a quarter of a turn back in the proper direction on the highway. It was as if an angel from heaven shoved our car out of harm's way. Stunned and amazed, I immediately worshiped the Lord in complete gratitude over His miraculous intervention. Utilizing our spiritual gear in the heat of the crisis will help us to have victory in Jesus's name.

Praying by faith in Jesus's name can move cars and mountains and heal the sick. Praying with grateful hearts is worship when we praise the Lord for His attributes. When we focus our worship on our Savior rather than ourselves, a confident peace comes over us. "Don't spend a lot of time describing your mountain to the Lord. He knows what it is. Instead, focus your attention on the mountain mover—His glory, power and faithfulness."[9] The Lord often answers our prayers in mysterious ways, either by a miracle or by working through fellow Christians.

Drawing Strength from One Another

As believers, we are stronger together than apart. Our triune Lord has created us to live in community and care for one another since we collectively represent the body of Christ. "If one part suffers, all the parts suffer with it, and if one part is honored, all the parts are glad. All of you together are Christ's body, and each of you is a part of it" (1 Corinthians 12:26 NLT). When believers function as a unified and harmonious team, we can draw strength from one another and overcome unexpected challenges along the trail.

An adventure in the Adirondack Mountains will leave a lasting impression with its epic views, mountain streams, stunning waterfalls, and a deep sense of accomplishment when you reach the summit of a 46er peak.. Even though I have hiked in beautiful places all over the world, I am constantly drawn back to unparalleled beauty of the High

Peaks in the Adirondacks. I resonate with John Muir's quote in his book *My First Summer in the Sierra*: "We are now in the mountains, and they are in us."[10] For generations, nature lovers and hikers from all over the country and world visit the Adirondacks to experience the incredible views from the summits of the forty-six High Peaks. The forty-six mountains have an altitude of 4,000 feet or above, and it is a hiking challenge that is hard to resist. I caught the "forty-sixer fever" years ago and decided to climb the highest peak.

I knew when I climbed Mount Marcy, the highest of the forty-sixers at 5,344 feet, it would become a metaphorical lesson somehow. I wasn't sure if the life lesson would be applicable to a personal mountain I had just come through or a challenging mountain yet to come.

Our hiking expedition team included my brother, Stephen, and longtime friend, Michelle. Eager to tackle the mountain early, we got up before the crack of dawn, ate a hearty breakfast, and finished packing our backpacks. Our excitement was palpable, as we struck a confident pose for a photo with our arm muscles flexed and huge smiles across our faces.

Just before we left the camp, my mother gave me a handful of Advil to keep in my pocket, and Dad handed Stephen a small flashlight. Only God could have known the gear we would need. Without Advil, a flashlight, and each other, the day would have ended up very differently.

While we drove to the trailhead in the heart of the Adirondacks, we sipped hot coffee and sang worship songs at the top of our lungs. The beautiful rainbow over the Adirondack Loj base lodge was a reassurance of His covenant blessing of peace for our trek. We did not know what the day held for us, but we were confident the Lord would go before us.

We hit the trail a little after 8:00 a.m. and cheerfully made our way into the heart of the wilderness. Our spirits remained high despite the unfortunate loss of Michelle's water from a leaky Nalgene water bottle. Even the pouring rain and the cold dampness that clung to our clothes afterward could not dampen our spirits. Our hiking adventure took us over suspended rope bridges, dense forest, and beautiful vistas. A thick cloud covering hovered over the mountains for the entire morning until we reached the summit. It was as if the Lord synchronized our summiting Mount Marcy with the sun bursting through the dark clouds. The magnificent, intense rays poured light onto the breathtaking 360-degree view of the forty-six High Peaks. We unanimously agreed this extraordinary view made the long vertical climb totally worth it.

Hikers have a wonderful camaraderie on the trails. People are eager to help one another and share stories along the way. One family we met at Marcy's summit consisted of five boys and their parents. It was the husband's forty-sixth birthday, and after he climbed Mount Marcy, he became an official forty-sixer! We were inspired by his story, which fueled our aspiration to climb other forty-sixer mountains.

After our lunch break at the summit, our muscles began to stiffen from hiker's fatigue. When I stood up, my right knee was tender and a little swollen. I must have unknowingly overextended it when I had to scramble up a rock face near the top. However, the full extent of the damage wasn't evident until I started my descent of the mountain. With every step down the steep trail, my knee pain dramatically increased.

I was thankful when Michelle wrapped my knee with an Ace bandage and carried my backpack. Stephen found a walking stick in the woods to support my weight as I limped down the trail. Out of desperation, I consumed more Advil than was advisable to bring down the swelling. I was determined to get down the mountain before nightfall. Our joking and laughing took a more serious tone when our water supply dried up and the daylight hours waned. Michelle initiated God's help by laying hands on my swollen knee and praying for His healing power to strengthen me. Miraculously, the pain in my knee greatly reduced, which eased my mobility.

Exhausted and dangerously dehydrated, hiking the last two miles in the pitch-black darkness of night felt like an eternity. It was a struggle for all of us not to succumb to fear. If it were not for Dad's flashlight, we would have gotten lost. Our anxiety grew when the trail began to look unfamiliar, and we debated if we should retrace our steps or continue forward. It was a pivotal moment, so we prayed together for God's guidance and decided to stay the course. It was a glorious moment when we finally reached my old blue Subaru in the parking lot.

Our Mount Marcy trek was certainly a memorable adventure. God provided all the necessary equipment for us all along the way. Even the smallest of details came together, reassuring us that God knows all our needs. Throughout the trek, we learned how to support one another in Christian community with encouragement, prayer, and the ministry of presence. These are pieces of our spiritual gear we cannot take for granted. We are created to bear one another's burdens and show kindness when someone is suffering from an injury of any kind. The Lord did not intend for us to climb our personal mountains alone. We are designed for relationship with one another and with our Lord. "Carry each other's burdens, and in this way, you will fulfill the law of Christ" (Galatians 6:2 NIV). Authentic relationships require us to love much, forgive much, and bear one another's burdens.

Loving Anyway

The Holy Spirit's job is to change a person's heart, and our job is to love them, not judge them, through the process. This is another strategy the Lord taught me when faced with spiritual opposition. God's Word gives us a command: "Beloved, if God so loved us, we also ought to love one another" (1 John 4:11 ESV). I've learned that I cannot change people, but I can change how I respond to their offenses. The principle of loving anyway is a spiritual weapon that can diffuse almost any situation. "A gentle answer turns away wrath, but a harsh word stirs up anger" (Proverbs 15:1 NIV).

It was a particularly difficult season when I was living with someone who was chronically critical, habitually ungrateful, and downright cutting with his words. One day, my patience ran out, and I had to take a walk outside to cool down. I was venting to God while I walked.

I yelled out loud, "I *can't* do this anymore! How can you allow me to be treated this way day after day?"

Immediately, the Lord spoke to my heart and said two words to me, *Love anyway.*

I was stunned. "Love anyway? Really, Lord?" Tears began to flow down my cheeks. I knew He was right, but I felt overwhelmed. I pleaded for the Lord's help because I knew that I couldn't love this person with my own strength. First John 4:21 (ESV) says, "Whoever loves God must also love his brother." The Holy Spirit guided me moment by moment and step by step. It was a spiritual battle for my heart, and I had a choice to respond in anger or in love.

I utilized every piece of spiritual gear for protection, strength, and wisdom. When we are mocked and torn down by the people who are supposed to love us, we can love anyway with the Holy Spirit's power. We can remind ourselves Christ loves us and promises to be with us always. Love anyway is a powerful spiritual warfare motto to live by so we don't blow our Christian witness. "By this all people will know that you are my disciples, if you have love for one another" (John 13:35 ESV). Jesus said, "I tell you, her sins—and they are many—have been forgiven, so she has shown me much love. But a person who is forgiven little shows only a little love" (Luke 7:47 NLT). I don't know about you, but I want my life and legacy to be shaped by forgiveness and love.

Choosing Forgiveness

Wearing the armor of God is essential to achieving victory on the battlefield of forgiveness. There is a war being waged for our souls. It is a real test of living out the gospel daily when we forgive people's cruel words, hateful attitudes, and contemptible actions, which cut deeper than a knife. I understand this reality in a profound way. Unfortunately, I have a vast breadth of experience of how much it costs to forgive the unforgivable. Have you ever had someone take from you something that is irreplaceable? Have you dealt with the marital betrayal and deception of a chronically unfaithful spouse? Have you ever had an abusive person rob you of your dignity and self-worth? Have you lived with an alcoholic who squanders your savings? Have you had a coworker secretly sabotage your reputation while they pretended to be your friend? We all have battle stories we could share. "If in this world men persecute and slander you do not let this surprise or distress you, for this is for you no place of rest, but a battlefield."[11]

In my case, God was simply asking me to extend the same grace that I have been given through Christ to people who had betrayed me. To remain defiant in my unforgiveness is to say to God that my suffering is greater than what Christ suffered on the cross. How could I stand before Christ someday and look at His nail-pierced hands and say that His sacrifice on the cross was not good enough? That is what Jesus communicated to me when I was holding onto injustices. Can you relate at all? Have you wrestled with God about the snare of unforgiveness? How is that going?

Forgiveness is the key to freedom and spiritual victory. "Forgiveness is powerful and beneficial. When we forgive someone for hurting us, it frees us from feeling like victims or feeling we are under the person who hurt us."[12] The freedom of forgiveness changes the attitude and posture of our hearts, from a victim to a victor, and from oppressed to set free. However, if you respond in anger or retaliation, then Satan wins, and you lose.

Satan's war strategy is to drive a wedge between your relationship with God and with others. "We have lost the sense that we are at war and that is why we are so often defeated. It is not that Christians don't want to win. They don't even know they are at war!"[13] We have God's wisdom and the Holy Spirit's power to be an overcomer. If we suppressed our emotional wounds, they could likely develop into stress cracks in our shield of faith, giving Satan a spiritual foothold to create chaos. A spiritual foothold is an entrance point into our heart and mind where our faith or character is weak. Satan looks for weak areas in your life—your bad attitude, unforgiveness, sinful actions, sexual temptation, pride, wrong beliefs, divided relationships, and the profane words you speak. These are all entrance points for destruction, like a fiery arrow to destroy your Christian witness. "Witnessing for Christ is not something we turn on and off like a TV set, every believer is a witness at all times—either a good one or a bad one."[14] The world is watching to see how we will respond. When we choose to forgive, the ripple effect can change people's marriages, families, and entire communities.

Unforgiveness creates an island of isolation and division, while forgiveness builds a bridge toward community and harmony. The helmet of salvation reminds us that God forgave us so we can forgive others.

Many years ago, a horrific crime rocked the nation and put the word *forgiveness* on everyone's lips. We watched the evening news in horror as we learned about a gunman who entered an Amish schoolhouse in Pennsylvania. He killed five little girls and wounded five others before he took his own life. Although everyone was grieved by this evil atrocity, the shooting spree was not the most surprising part of the story. Even the most sanctified of Christians were amazed by the Amish community's kindness to the family of the deceased gunman. They immediately responded with Christlike forgiveness despite his heinous crime of killing their precious little girls. As a community, the Amish families attended the funeral of the gunman, hugged his family, and brought them food. They showed extraordinary grace and compassion in the face of their own painful loss.

> *Unforgiveness creates an island of isolation and division, while forgiveness builds a bridge toward community and harmony.*

Why did this genuine display of Christ's forgiveness shock the nation? Because most people demand justice in the face of injustice. The insatiable thirst for justice can overshadow the command to follow Christ's example of love, grace, and forgiveness. The Amish community forgave because they took the commands in God's Word seriously. In Matthew 6:14–15 (NLT), Jesus said, "If you forgive those who sin against you, your heavenly Father will forgive you. But if you refuse to forgive others, your Father will not forgive your sins." The Amish community's forgiveness was genuine and compassionate. It was only through the power of the Holy Spirit that they could forgive the unforgivable. When faith and difficult life circumstances collide, how we respond reflects the strength of our shield of faith and how well we understand the gospel. The Amish showed love to the gunman's family because they understood that Christ first loved them while they were still sinners. Their helmet of salvation was secure, which empowered them to pass on the forgiveness they had been given by Christ.

Forgiveness is a decision and a process that leads to transformational healing. There are many layers to forgiving frequent offenses and stages of letting go. Let the sword of the Spirit, God's Word, cut through the heartbreak and damaging lies. Forgiveness is like cutting an onion; each new layer brings tears, but it also brings you to a deeper level of faith. When you ask the Lord to help you to forgive, the Holy Spirit will carefully remove all hidden layers of decay and bitterness in your soul so you can truly heal. Expect the tears and allow yourself to have a good cry to let out all the suppressed emotions. The Holy Spirit will show you how to let go of the hurt so you can be victorious on the battlefield of forgiveness.

Life Lessons Learned

The Holy Spirit fuels our spiritual strength. The spiritual battles we face are not temporary but lifelong. The bolder we are for Christ, the more the battle will intensify. God's Word tells us that during the last days, Christ followers will be persecuted. Do not fear, for God has given us all we need to stand firm and faithful until the end. The Lord is with us.

We are all broken people; we are just broken in different places. What unifies all of us is our need for hope and healing, which is why we need to share Christ's good news with others. During these tumultuous times in our society, the spiritual battle is rampant. You may feel knocked down right now, but it is imperative to get up and keep sharing your faith. Our battle is not against flesh and blood but against powers and principalities. When faced with hateful words and actions, we defuse the power of evil over us when we respond by loving people anyway. People will know we are Christians by our love. Loving others well will bring glory to God, especially when there is sacrifice involved. The Lord is the ultimate judge and jury, and one day (hopefully soon) He will make all things new again.

In this world filled with suffering, it is easy to feel weighed down by the sheer magnitude of injustices all around us. If we fail to make use of our spiritual gear, our emotions can come unhinged in the heat of battle. For example, take the issue of forgiveness. If we apply our spiritual gear and forgive much, then Satan can't get a foothold and divide relationships. However, if we fail to forgive, then unforgiveness and bitterness will turn into an obstructive boulder that can block us from God's narrow path. The way to press on through spiritual battles is to activate the power of the Holy Spirit. He will enable us to utilize the armor of God by releasing strongholds that bind us, wielding God's Word, remembering the powerful name of Jesus Christ, embracing our Christian community, loving people anyway, and choosing to forgive. Rest assured; the Lord has equipped us to live a victorious life.

CLIMB THE MOUNTAIN
SCENE 5

After a steep ascent through a rocky section of the trail, I was growing tired, so I decided to pace myself. I sat down next to a huge glacial erratic. There was a groove cut out of the rock which made it a perfect place to rest and reflect. Glacial erratic boulders are scattered throughout the many hiking trails in the Adirondack Mountains. Long ago, the boulders were dragged by the glacier ice and moved to a totally different land and left there when the ice melted. Scientists can tell because the rock substance is radically different from all the other rocks in the location where it now stands. The word *erratic* is a Latin word, which means "to go astray." The Merriam-Webster dictionary defines erratic as "wandering."[1] How appropriate. Our emotional boulders can also cause us to go astray if we are not careful. Reflecting on my life journey, I could see how my emotional boulders had caused me to wander off trail for a season until the Holy Spirit redirected me. God's mercies are renewed every morning, and He wants us to press on past the boulders in our path.

While resting my foot, I redirected my thoughts to one of God's promises, "I can do all things through Christ who strengthens me" (Philippians 4:13 NASB). This verse reassured me that Christ's strength is more than enough for me to press on despite my injury. I asked the Holy Spirit to renew my resolve with this powerful promise. I rose to my feet and noticed the other side of the boulder sloping down in the back where a large yellow birch tree was growing strong and tall with abundant leaves on its branches. The roots were contorted at an angle.

Half of the roots were on the rock and a few had traveled downward into the rich soil. Despite the barrenness and the struggle of being planted on the side of a boulder, the tree trunk had continued to grow straight and tall, reaching for the sunlight. The birch tree's canopy of leaves was vibrantly healthy and did not show any signs of decay. This was such a striking illustration of pressing onward and growing upward toward the Son-light of Jesus Christ despite obstacles and opposition in our lives.

Like a salve, this powerful metaphor ministered to my broken heart and gave me renewed inspiration to move forward, not only on the hike, but in life as well. Over my lifetime, I have known the greatest joy of authentic Christian community, and I have also experienced the intense sorrow of isolation and loneliness. I will never forget what my friend said to me while sitting at his kitchen table one day. He said, "Sharon, being isolated and alone is exactly where Satan wants you to be right now. You need to take steps to trust again and enter back into Christian community. Only then will you experience the fullness of what God has for you." I pondered his comments for a long time. In God's strength, I got back up and decided to press on past the sting of betrayal and take steps to trust again.

CHAPTER 5

PRESSING ON PAST THE BOULDERS

I press on toward the goal for the prize of the heavenly call of God in Christ Jesus.

Philippians 3:14 NRSV

The Race Called Endurance

People who participate in extreme sports simultaneously amaze and perplex me. I wish I could be an intense athlete, but the amount of time it takes to train for those events is staggering. I have so little time of my own these days that it is hard to fathom. If I did have extra time, I would rather go for a long hike up another forty-sixer mountain in the ADR (Adirondack Mountain Club), travel, or write prose at my favorite coffee shop.

But intense athletes inspire me every time I watch them at a race. I'm the person on the sidelines cheering competitors on as they run by. I have attended several Chicago marathons and used to enjoy sipping my Starbucks coffee on the sidelines, yelling, "Woo-hoo, you're doing great!" then chomping another bite out of my cider donut. I would shout with the utmost enthusiasm, "Way to go!" then wash the dough-nut down with my coffee and wipe the crumbs from my face with my napkin. I know I'll never be a marathon runner, but I think I would enjoy being a marathon doughnut eater someday.

It seems as if extreme sports are everywhere in the Adirondacks. I wonder if God especially created the people who live here to fearlessly ski off jumps, participate in Ironman races, become winter Olympians, show horses, mountain bike, white water raft, or participate in the 90-Miler, the Adirondack Canoe Classic race. I marvel at the intense physical exertion that a body can endure. I once watched the three-day 90–Miler and cheered the paddlers on as they crossed the finish line at Lake Flower in Saranac Lake, New York. I did not have any coffee or doughnuts in my hand that time, only my cell phone and a mini notebook to scribble my writer notes. I watched as the second-to-last canoe crossed the finish line paddled by a smiling man in his late sixties. *Good for him,* I thought. *Go ahead, defy age, my friend!*

I studied the crowd and noticed quite a few people my age and older, but very few kids. In fact, I saw only one boy, age seven, who participated in this race. The seven-year-old was part of the paddler boat which had three generations: a grandpa, father, and son team. What a great memory this will be for them as a family.

I feel right at home with the North Country folks, who are passionate about exploring the beauty of the mountains and lakes while also being intentional about the preservation of the "forever wild" land. ADKers are fiercely independent people known for their hard work ethic and entrepreneurial spirit. Paddling the 90-Miler takes an incredible amount of perseverance and hard work. I loved standing there, cheering everyone on, and being a part of the celebratory finishes.

Just then I noticed two women with wringing wet hair and clothes, who were sitting on the ground eating the hot celebration meal that was served for paddlers at the end of the race. Heavy rain had poured during the last few days, and I'm sure they were chilled—you know, the kind of coldness that chills to the bone until your teeth chatter and you wonder if you will ever be warm again. *Brrrrr.* I shivered out of compassion, instantly thankful for my extra-thick hooded sweatshirt and North Face raincoat.

When I asked the young women if this was their first race, they both smiled and proudly showed me their calloused and blistered hands. I asked if they would do it again, and the first one to speak exclaimed, "Absolutely!" while the other remained silent. After a few moments of awkward silence, we all broke out in laughter. Silence sometimes speaks louder than words, doesn't it? I guess she'd had enough paddling for a lifetime.

In addition to ninety miles of river and lakes to paddle on, there are also several miles of portages where people had to carry their boats up to a mile in between lakes. The racecourse follows some of the original Adirondack water roads traversed by Adirondack guides, Native Americans, and early settlers. This particular year, the 90-Miler race has 250 boats and around 500 paddlers who started the race from Old Forge Pond through the Fulton Chain, the Eckford Chain, Long Lake, Raquette River, and through the Saranac Lakes. Considering I have only paddled five miles around the circumference of Lake Titus, I am fully aware that I would need to have a long season to train before I could participate in the 90-Miler race. I wonder, would they allow me to bring doughnuts along for energy?

All races in life are optional except the life race called endurance. You do not choose this race, but rather this race chooses you whether you feel prepared or not. It is the most extreme sport you will ever participate in. You're not sure what to expect with the tough terrain, and each turn presents an unexpected boulder or obstacle. *But* there is good news. "May the Lord lead your hearts into a full understanding and expression of the love of God and the patient endurance that comes from Christ" (2 Thessalonians 3:5 NLT). God knows the sovereign trail map, and He has provided the proper gear. Jesus is your fearless Adirondack guide and trainer, and your comforter is the Holy Spirit. Our triune God has promised to never leave you nor forsake you. God has already decided that after you cross the finish line, He will give you the highest prize of spending eternal life in heaven with Him! If that doesn't fire you up to run the race with endurance, then I have to check your pulse. Isn't that wonderful? You will end up in the most glorious place for all eternity if you have a personal relationship with Christ.

The endurance trail is full of boulders that block your path, roots that try to trip you up, and performance pain that reminds you of your dependence upon God. The race is not all drudgery, as there are sweet moments where you feel pure joy as you run the race of life that has been uniquely designed for you. It is in those moments that you are grateful God created you to live in His freedom. I love what Rick Warren said in his book, *The Purpose Driven Life*: "The secret of endurance is to remember that your pain is temporary, but your reward will be eternal."[1] If you ask athletes what keeps them going during the race, they will often tell you they visualized the moment of pure joy when they cross the finish line.

There was an extraordinary woman named Grace Hudowalksi, who was the first woman to climb all the forty-sixers. She was a strong, feisty woman with a spirit of adventure. Her passion and love for the Adirondacks is why she became the local ADK forty-sixer hiking historian and collected thousands of letters that hikers mailed in about their adventures. On her first climb to Mount Marcy's summit, she said, "It was tough. I was on all fours sometimes. I didn't think I was going to get there. But I had to get to the top—there was some reason. God knows what it was but I had to go on. And on the top just for a fraction of a moment, the clouds lifted while I was there and I looked down and there a mile below me was Lake Tear of the Clouds, the Hudson River's highest source. And you know, that did something to me. I had seen something—I felt it. I never forgot the mountain and I never forgot that trip."[2] I can relate to Grace and her experience.

I know what it feels like to have to get down on all fours just to keep going. The betrayal I endured nearly crushed my heart. Have you ever seen a boulder break off a mountain and literally crush all life in its path? Betrayal feels like a crushing blow that knocks your breath out. It makes you feel like giving up, like packing up and going home. But God calls us to move forward and heavenward, even if it means we have to scramble on all fours to reach the summit.

As believers, we never forget the trials on the journey that God brings us through. God helps us to press on, especially when life gets hard. Our trials become part of our cross story, our personal testimony to God's goodness and grace. "So let your lives preach, let your light shine, that your works may be seen, that your Father may be glorified."[3] If we keep our eyes fixed on the prize of eternal life and allow the joy and anticipation of heaven to give us the will to press on each day, we can overcome our boulders and receive all He has promised us.

"So do not throw away this confident trust in the Lord. Remember the great reward it brings you! Patient endurance is what you need now, so that you will continue to do God's will. Then you will receive all that he has promised. For in just a little while, the Coming One will come and not delay" (Hebrews 10:35–37). Remember, "God's purpose in your life is not to make everything easy. Our lives are meant to have meaning."[4] A meaningful life comes from learning from our mistakes, growing in Christlikeness, and forgiving the unforgiveable offenses.

Unforgiveness Is a Heavy Burden

"When transgressions rip apart relationships, forgiveness is the seam-stress who reweaves the jagged tear in trust, thread by thread."[5] When we ask the Holy Spirit to do spiritual inventory of the condition of our hearts, He is faithful to free us from the hidden sins, like unforgiveness, that weigh us down.

The heavy burden of unforgiveness is like a novice backpacker with too much equipment in their pack. Can you visualize a back-packer that looks like they are bent over carrying a huge boulder on their back? We were not meant to carry such a heavy load. My brother, Stephen and I took a trip of a lifetime when we hiked the four-day and three-night mountain trek in Peru. We hiked through cloud forests, rainforests, and ancient Mayan ruins on the legendary Inca Trail to Machu Picchu. I vividly remember trying to get my backpack down to only twenty pounds because the high altitude of the Andes Mountains would make my backpack feel like forty.

Carrying extra weight in your backpack is similar to how life works with holding on to unforgiveness. The weight of the burden only intensifies over time until you feel buried underneath it. I'll never forget when I forgave my ex-husband in the lawyer's office on the last day of our divorce agreement. Despite how horribly I was treated during the meeting, I knew that I must speak a word of forgiveness to him at the end when no one else was around. I forgave him for his repeated lying and unfaithfulness and wished him God's best for his life. He was not expecting me to say those words after such a harsh meeting, and he broke down in tears and asked if he could hug me. I said yes with tears in my eyes, and I asked him to forgive me too. Healing tears flowed when we honestly forgave one other, and I felt like I had a thousand pounds lifted off my back.

It was profoundly life changing to experience the freedom and healing of forgiveness with my ex-husband and with other family members right before I went into full-time church ministry. The Lord freed me of the heavy burden I was carrying so I could help others navigate the complexities of forgiveness. Forgiveness is an essential part of our gear because without it we will get spiritually tripped up by the oppressive weight.

We are hypocrites if we claim to love God while we hate our brother or sister. The passage in 1 John 4:20 (NLT) says, "If someone says, 'I love God' but hates a fellow believer, that person is a liar; for if we don't love the people we can see, how can we love God, whom we cannot see?" We cannot fully love God and our neighbor if the poison of hatred and anger is harbored in our hearts. It will consume you and derail you from being kingdom minded.

Unforgiveness is a bad root, and it can yield a deadly fruit of bitterness that will harden your heart. "Get rid of all bitterness, rage, anger, and harsh words, and slander, as well as all types of evil behavior. Instead, be kind to each other, tender hearted, forgiving one another, just as God through Christ has forgiven you" (Ephesians 4:31–32 NLT).

When we choose not to forgive, it hurts us and our relationship with God more than it hurts the offender. Unforgiveness limits our ability to love deeply. In the gospel of Luke, when the prostitute kissed and poured perfume on Jesus's feet and wiped His feet with her hair, it was an incredibly moving moment. Jesus replied to all the Pharisees who were showing disgust toward her, "'I tell you, her sins—and they are many—have been forgiven, so she has shown me much love. But a person who is forgiven little shows only little love.' Then Jesus said to the woman, 'Your sins are forgiven'" (Luke 7:47–48 NLT). There is a direct correlation between repentance, forgiveness, and the ability to love much.

God wants us to clean out the boulders in our unforgiving hearts through repentance before we ask Him for other things in prayer. "I tell you, you can pray for anything, and if you believe that you've received it, it will be yours. But when you are praying, first forgive anyone you are holding a grudge against, so that your Father in heaven will forgive your sins, too" (Mark 11:24–26 NLT).

When we have been transformed by the gospel and have been touched by God's lavish grace and forgiveness, we, in turn, want to share that grace and forgiveness with others. "Our generous and constant forgiveness of others should be the natural result of our embracing the forgiveness God has extended to us."[6] I would dare to say that if you are a Christian and refuse to forgive, it's possible you have forgotten the depth of the sin that Christ has forgiven you. Forgiveness is not an optional command. Charles Swindoll states it well: "Forgiveness is not an elective in the curriculum of servanthood. It is a required course, and the exams are always tough to pass."[7] Our enemy's sin is not worse than our own sin. Therefore, we must never forget that Christ forgave you and me, so we can forgive others.

Authentic forgiveness is a kind of surrender that proclaims, *God is the judge and jury, and I am not! God is in control and I am not!* Once I surrender the outcome and the justice to the Lord, it is actually quite freeing. It is God's job to exact justice, not mine. My job is to forgive, surrender justice, and show mercy. Jesus tells us, "Blessed are the merciful, for they shall receive mercy" (Matthew 5:7 NLT).

When you forgive, God cuts loose the bondage of unforgiveness and severs the heavy chains that bind you to that person. Releasing unforgiveness brings greater freedom. Christ-centered forgiveness is unconditional and, therefore, does not depend on the offender's change of heart. The balm of forgiveness frees your heart to begin to heal, and it turns the situation over to God's hands to exact justice in His timing. "Vengeance is mine, I will repay, says the Lord" (Romans 12:19 ESV). You can come to God with all the ways people have offended and sinned against you. He will lift the thousand-pound boulder of unforgiveness that has kept you pinned down and immobilized. The destructive power of unforgiveness can enslave your thought life, rob you of joy, and cause you to say hurtful things. Asking God to cleanse you from the festering wounds of unforgiveness will free you more than you can ever imagine. "If we confess our sins to him, he is faithful and just to forgive us our sins and to cleanse us from all wickedness" (1 John 1:9 NLT).

Won't you lay your ultra-heavy backpack of unforgiveness down at the foot of the cross? Begin by telling Jesus, *I give my pain as an offering to you*. You can start with a simple prayer:

Lord, help me to forgive the person(s) [fill in the blank] who hurt me so profoundly. You are a God who heals, and I trust you to do a miraculous work in my heart. I know you are the God of justice and righteousness, and I release this person(s) and the situation into your trustworthy hands. Blessed be your name, Jesus. Amen."

We bring glory to our heavenly Father when we forgive the most heinous of crimes against us and our loved ones. Corrie ten Boom said it perfectly, "Yes, we never touch the ocean of God's love as much as when we love our enemies. It is such a joy to accept forgiveness, but it is almost a greater joy to give forgiveness."[8] Forgiveness communicates to the unbelieving world that we have an inner strength to do the impossible because of Christ's work in our hearts and lives. Jesus is the only explanation. The power of this kind of testimony is appealing and fragrant, which will attract people to want to know more about Jesus when they face their own personal storms.

Fix Our Eyes on Jesus in the Storm

When I traveled to Israel with a group from my Chicago church, we had the privilege of sailing on an old wooden boat into the heart of the Sea of Galilee. The winds were calm that day, and the sun glistened on the waves as our boat glided through the waters. I was struck by how small the Sea of Galilee was as I could see the shore on all sides with raised hills in the background. The shape of the landscape reminded me of being in a bowl with the sea in the middle. Our seasoned sea captain explained that the weather can turn in an instant, which explains why the disciples were caught off guard that day when Jesus walked on the water to them in the boat. As we sailed across the smooth waters, I listened to Matthew 14:22–32 being read aloud. The biblical story came to life in a fresh way to all of us.

The Scripture passage doesn't tell us how long the storm had been raging, but we do know the disciples had been fighting heavy waves until the middle of the night. It was 3:00 a.m. when Jesus came to them over the water. I can only imagine the disciples' reactions. They were utterly exhausted, rain-soaked, and probably very hungry; I'm sure they were wondering if they could even trust their blurry eyes at that moment. They made out what looked like a ghost coming toward them, and fear paralyzed them. Jesus, in His reassuring voice, said, "Take courage and be not afraid." Jesus didn't mind when Peter asked for reassurance. He said, "Come to me, Peter!"

I visualize Peter reaching out his open hands toward Jesus as he stepped out of the boat without any awareness of what the disciples were thinking about him, the raging storm, or the fact that he was actually walking on water. Peter fearlessly fixed his eyes on Jesus and placed one foot in front of the other. However, the moment Peter looked away from Christ's eyes, the bottom of his faith dropped out, and he began to sink into a dark abyss filled with fear. When Peter cried out to his Lord to save him, Jesus immediately reached down and pulled Peter up.

Out of frustration, Jesus asked Peter, "Why do you have such little faith?" as if to imply, *After all that I have taught and shown you, why do you still doubt Me? Peter, how can you doubt Me when you have witnessed the Father work through Me time and time again?* I imagine Jesus still holding Peter's hand as they entered the boat together. In

Christ's omnipotent power, the wind instantly halted the minute He entered the boat. In that moment, the disciples recognized Christ's holiness in contrast to their humanity, which compelled them to fall on their faces to worship the Son of the living God!

I, too, am renewed with awe and want to get on my knees and worship the Lord for His complete holiness, His complete compassion, and His complete mercy upon me. How awesome, mighty, powerful, and miraculous is the Lord God Almighty. Just as He did for the disciples, Christ patiently reassures us during our own critical crisis moments.

We can learn many key principles from Matthew 14 to apply to our own difficult circumstances on how to press on past our metaphorical boulders. First, Jesus *told* the disciples to get in the boat and cross the sea. Taking the boat across the Sea of Galilee was Jesus's idea, not the disciples'. Sometimes we feel as though a difficult situation was avoidable or that we missed God's leading and that is why we find ourselves in a boatload of trouble. That might be true some of the time, but it is not true all the time. We simply cannot control every aspect of our lives to avoid all of life's hurts. Sometimes our hardship is preplanned, God-ordained suffering that He uses to build our character and strengthen our faith.

Second, Christ, in His infinite compassion and mercy, came to the disciples and reassured them. Jesus did not abandon or forsake the disciples; He comforted them and rescued them in their darkest hour of need. He will do the same for us.

Third, Jesus is sovereign over all of creation, which is demonstrated by the fact that Jesus walked on water and silenced the heavy winds the very instant He spoke. When we are in the presence of Christ, we do not need to fear anything. Choose faith over fear.

Fourth, Peter was bold and courageous. I think Peter gets the short straw in the way that people focus on his failure in this story instead of his bold faith that preceded his wavering. Peter had tremendous faith. Peter knew that Christ could enable him to walk on the water, but he waited for Christ's command. When God calls us, we can trust that He will embolden us with courage.

Fifth, Peter boldly stepped out of his comfort zone of the boat. Was staying inside the boat safer than walking on water with Jesus? I believe it is safer to take a bold risk under Christ's command and authority than it is to stay in a man-made boat. I would choose to take Jesus by the hand any day! Like Peter, when we are sinking into the dark abyss, all we can do is cry out a simple prayer of faith—*Jesus, save me*—and He is immediately present with us. It does not mean that we immediately get taken out of the sea and placed into a luxury yacht. Jesus is present with us in the storm. He gives us His hand, and He will lift us up. We can trust Him. "Imagine what your life will look like when you have broken the bondage of fear."[9] Don't you love that quote by Bruce Wilkinson? I do. When we focus on the Father and not on our own fears, He can accomplish great things in us and through us.

God may not rescue us from our painful circumstance, but He does promise to help us persevere through it. He is greater than any storm that comes your way, even death. "No storm is so great, no wave is so high, no sea is so deep, no wind is so strong, that Jesus cannot either calm it or carry us through it."[10] So keep calm and press on. Remember, when God doesn't move our mountain, He will give us faith to climb it. The Psalms are filled with honest laments, but they are also filled with faith and hope that God delivers, God rescues, and God is our strong tower. "Though I walk in the midst of trouble, you will revive me; you will stretch forth your hand against the wrath of my enemies and your right hand will save me" (Psalm 138:7 NASB).

Eternal Peace

Looking at my grandma's frail ninety-pound frame in the hospital bed was like looking at a skeleton with a thin piece of flesh draped over it. It brought me to tears as I looked at the purple and black bruises on her legs and arms that were a side effect of her dialysis. Her fingers and toes had turned a bright shade of blue because of poor circulation, and her body looked weary. The needles and tubes coming out of her hand and chest pained me as I saw the discomfort they caused her. Sweet Grandma looked so fragile in her ninety-sixth year of life, and her hand shook as she reached up to touch her face. There was much to absorb and process. Hospital noises circulated around the sacred space with transfusion instruments beeping, nurses scurrying around, and her roommate's TV blasting at full volume.

My cousin served as our pastor that day, and he brought us together as a family to take communion. There must have been twenty-five of us who formed a lopsided circle around Grandma's hospital bed. We partook of the cup and the bread together, and my cousin emphasized the importance of family. As he encouraged us through his words, tears came to our eyes, and we closed with prayer. When we left to go our separate ways, I wondered if all of us would ever be gathered that way again. Grandma was the glue in our family. In her quiet, loving way, she brought everyone together for holidays and special occasions.

I watched my dad's face and observed how his eyes were filled with agonizing grief. How difficult it must have been to see his own mother in such a frail and weakened state. He fought off tears and walked away, stating out loud, "She is going to live to be a hundred." Later that day, during a lucid moment, Grandma told me very adamantly that she was "*not* going to live to be a hundred." With a glint in her eye, she reassured me, "But I know where I am going."

So we began to talk about heaven. As I read to her the Scriptures about heaven, our hearts filled with joyful expectation. We happily discussed how the streets will be lined with gold, the leaves of the trees would be used for healing, and how Christ will make all things new again. The people sitting at the heavenly banquet table would include her husband, parents, siblings, and her son Glen, who had died when he was seventeen. We talked about how she was going to be skipping and laughing, free from needles and tubes. And the praise music—well, it would be beyond her wildest dreams! Grandma loved praise music, and our family loves to sing and worship together. She smiled and said, "Sharon, you're going to be there with me too."

I replied, "Yes, Grandma, someday I'll be there with you too." She leaned back and went into a deep sleep as I sat quietly by her bed.

I sat in the hospital room and watched Grandma for hours. Her very life seemed to slowly slip away with each minute that passed. Suddenly, I saw her lifeless face come alive, filled with light as her expression became one of joy and amazement. Her eyes were open, and she was looking straight up at the ceiling with arms outstretched. I wondered if she was looking at her Creator, as her face looked so peaceful and serene. She was talking in a barely audible whisper at a rapid pace as if she was asking Him all the questions she had wondered about in her lifetime.

My aunt said, "It is as if Grandma is living in two separate worlds right now." She was not fully present in this world or the next, but she had God's peace. It was a fleeting moment, but the memory is permanently etched in my mind. "God's peace can break through the bleakest of circumstances, even into those moments when we stare into darkness and the shadow of death."[11] That is how I will remember these last days with Grandma, her glorious glimpses of heaven and conversations with God.

Heaven is what we get to look forward to someday, and it is our reason for persevering past life's unexpected boulders. Having an eternal perspective will allow us to see our Transformational Trek through the mountaintops and valleys as an adventure with God. Each one of us has a purpose greater than our own comfort. "Do not underestimate the role you may play in clearing the obstacles in someone's spiritual journey."[12] We are called to be witnesses, and the Lord will provide opportunities for the ministry of the unexpected. Oftentimes, people are most receptive to hearing about Jesus when they are emotionally broken and dealing with heartbreak. The Lord delights in giving us His peace like a river as He helps us to press on and glide past our boulders.

Peace like a River

After a long drive down a dirt road that seemingly led to nowhere, my brother, Stephen, and I came to the turnoff point for our favorite hidden waterfall that was part of the Salmon River. Unless you heard by word of mouth from the local people about the falls, you might not know about this breathtaking jewel deep in the forest. We grabbed our backpacks and headed down the muddy path with great expectation. The trail followed the river as we walked over hand-hewn log bridges and wooded pine trails. The verse from Isaiah 66, "peace like a river," popped into my head as I gazed down the Big Salmon River. One might think that peace like a river translates to a quiet or gentle river, but that is often not the case in the Adirondacks. I observed the river at different points along the trail. It had twists and turns, sometimes fast and other times slower rapids, and occasionally the river would become so calm you could see the fish on the bottom.

On this particular river, the water was calm as glass right before it turned into a major waterfall. Just like life, right? Our lives can sometimes be incredibly peaceful right before an unexpected, life-altering circumstance drops us down a waterfall with smashing force and intensity. Prayer is what keeps us afloat. Max Lucado beautifully writes, "Believing prayer ushers in God's peace. Not a random, nebulous, earthly peace, but His peace. Imported from heaven. The same tranquility that marks the throne room, God offers to you."[13] Our Sovereign Lord can still give us internal peace through believing prayer during the descent into unforeseen tumultuous waters and hidden boulders.

My brother and I climbed up to the highest point on the rock cliff that overhangs the waterfalls. To keep in line with our family tradition, we started a small fire to roast our red-hot Glazier hot dogs, which are an Adirondack culinary specialty, I might add. Their red color and spicy taste sets Glazier dogs apart from ordinary hot dogs. They are *the* dogs of all hot dogs! While Stephen tended the crackling fire, I walked down to the base of the river to capture this moment in my journal. I sat on moss-covered rocks and looked up at the yellow birch trees bending over the river as if they were leaning in to catch a better view. Some of the trees grew so close together, it looked as if their arms were interwoven around each other creating a natural archway.

The sunlight flickered and danced through the leaves and illumined various hues of yellow and lime green against the dark green backdrop of the forest. The play of light and shadow enhanced the rich visual experience of being in the deep woods. The roar of the mountain river was almost deafening as the water forcefully broke against the rocks, spraying in all directions. The iron minerals turned the water into a coffee color, which contrasted the latte-colored foam that formed at the base of the waterfall. I watched how the river forcibly slammed into the boulders but kept propelling forward toward a destination unknown.

The metaphorical boulders in our lives might stop us at first, but we don't have to remain stuck there clinging to the boulder for dear life. No, we need to get off the rock and trust God enough to continue moving forward with holy boldness. We need to remember that we have the peace of Christ living inside us. "With God's peace, we can stand firm in distress, disease, destruction, and even death."[14] We can have peace knowing that even the boulders of life are part of God's divine plan for preparing us for something greater in the future.

Resolve to Press On

We never know what boulders will come rolling into our lives, when, or with what intensity. A boulder that hit my aunt's life was a diagnosis of pancreatic cancer, and she was given only a few months to live. Our extended family gathered to encourage her with a prayer service in her home. I felt so blessed to be part of such a rich spiritual heritage of various denominations and different worship styles. We are unified with spiritual oneness through the gospel of Jesus Christ.

One of the sweetest memories I have of my aunt toward the end of her life was when the peace of the Lord filled our hearts as we quietly sang together. One evening, I asked my aunt the name of her favorite worship song, and she said, "It Is Well with My Soul." Her daughter quickly went to the computer and pulled up several music artists who had performed that song. We listened to Chris Rice sing "It Is Well with My Soul" three times before going to bed that night. The truth of the lyrics ministered to all our hearts. After my aunt went home to be with the Lord, her children appropriately selected that song for the funeral service. As I sang the lyrics, it was such a reassurance to me that it *was well with her soul* because of her personal relationship with Christ.

I felt compelled to read about the backstory of this powerful song; you may have heard it. "It Is Well with My Soul" was written by Horatio Spafford in 1873. The hymn was born out of great suffering when he financially lost everything, and then several of his children tragically died. The Great Chicago Fire of 1871 swept the city and burned down his property investments along Lake Michigan. Two years later, Horatio planned to travel by boat to Europe. His work detained him, but his family went ahead as planned on the steamship to Europe. It must have felt like a knife to his heart when he heard the news that the steamship *SS Ville du Havre* collided with another ship and sank to the bottom of the ocean, killing hundreds of people. Only a few survived by clinging to pieces of the wooden ship wreckage until a rescue boat arrived. Horatio received a telegram from his wife with the heartbreaking words, "Saved alone, what shall I do?" His wife had miraculously survived, but sadly, his four precious daughters drowned. Years later, Horatio and his wife were blessed with more children, and they moved to Jerusalem to start a mission to show the love of Christ to the poor, sick, and homeless children.

A crushed heart can be a catalyst for creativity.

Horatio Spafford's daughter Bertha wrote her book, *Our Jerusalem.* The following words describe her father's journey of suffering as he took the next ship across the Atlantic Ocean. The captain pointed out the spot where his four daughters died, and Horatio wrote his emotions in a letter to his wife, which was later recounted in his daughter's book.

> We passed over the spot where she went down in mid-ocean, the water three miles deep. But I do not think of our dear

ones there. They are safe, the dear lambs, and before very long, shall we be too. In the meantime, thanks to God, we have an opportunity to serve and praise Him for His love and mercy to us and ours. I will praise Him while I have my being. May we each one arise, leave all, and follow Him. To Father, this was a passing through the "valley of the shadow of death," but his faith came through triumphant and strong. On the high seas, near the place where his children perished, he wrote the hymn that was to give comfort to so many: That he could write such words at such a time was made possible by the fierceness of his struggle and the completeness of the victory.[15]

Horatio turned to God in his raw grief and poured out his devotion through writing the worship song "It Is Well with My Soul." Often when people go through a season of intense suffering, they can become inspired artists producing great art, music, poetry, and prose. A crushed heart can be a catalyst for creativity. Expressing oneself in an artistic outlet can be an important part of the healing process. "Perhaps we struggle to see the connection between worship and the call to be creative precisely because they are so intimately linked. We have forgotten that the call to creativity is a call to worship."[16] When we suffer, we can allow God to use the experience for His glory and praise Him through our pain. It reminds me of when everything had been taken away from Job—his children, servants, property, wealth, and health, and yet he said in Job 1:21 (ESV), "The Lord gave and the Lord has taken away; blessed be the name of the Lord!" Job worshiped God in his suffering, and so did Horatio. Both men were steadfast in their devotion to God despite their profound loss. Horatio did not allow this tragedy to cause him to turn away from Jesus. If anything, he clung more tightly to the cross

When we suffer, we can allow God to use the experience for His glory and praise Him through our pain.

for comfort and devoted his life to Christian ministry by serving the poor in Jerusalem.

The comfort of Christ is a soothing balm to our loneliness. "It seems to me that if we get one look at Christ in His love and beauty, this world and its pleasures will look very small to us."[17] After my divorce, I ran into the loving arms of Christ for comfort, and by His grace, He has sustained me all these years. Often after a marriage ends, people try to soothe their loneliness with another relationship, which could only leave them feeling emptier inside. After years of rejection in their unhealthy marriage, they desperately want to feel loved. Believe me, I get it! The temptation is real. My friends, "Keep your eyes open. You will be tempted."[18] But unless Jesus is the covenantal glue for the relationship, then it will only be a shadow of the real thing. The awful, never-ending process of combating temptation is God's means of maturing us and conforming us to the image of Christ."[19] We all have costly choices to make at the crossroads of life.

What choices will you make in your seasons of heartbreak? Will you run to Christ and worship Him even though there is intense pain in your heart? Or will you defiantly run away from Him to try and satisfy your own desires? God wants to comfort you and give you His peace. Isaiah 66:12 (ESV) says, "For thus says the Lord: 'I will extend peace to her like a river, and the glory of the nations like an overflowing stream; and you shall nurse, you shall be carried upon her hip, and bounced upon her knees. As one whom his mother comforts, so will I comfort you; and you shall be comforted over Jerusalem.'" The truth that we can hold onto with great confidence is that our intimacy with God is sweeter than any earthly relationship. In His arms, you can find lasting peace, devotion, and the security that you desire.

Life Lessons Learned

God is not surprised by any unexpected boulders—not a societal crisis, unexpected health diagnosis, or a traumatic experience. Nor was He taken off guard by a global pandemic virus, economic instability, or senseless violence. The Lord told us in the Scriptures about the coming persecution of the church, natural disasters, and turmoil. He foresaw this instability coming long ago and promised to be with us until the very end. No one knows when Christ will return, but we do know the signs that God gave in the Bible to indicate when the end draws near. Before Christ returns, "the love of most will grow cold but the one who stands firm to the end will be saved. And this gospel of the kingdom will be preached in the whole world as a testimony to all nations, and then the end will come" (Matthew 24:12–14 NIV).

As Christ followers, the Holy Spirit will give us the resolve to press on past the boulders and endure character refinement along the way. God will often use our boulders as part of His divine plan to sanctify us and teach us valuable life lessons. As Charles Spurgeon says, "Sanctification grows out of faith in Jesus Christ. Remember holiness is a flower, not a root; it is not sanctification that saves, but salvation that sanctifies."[20] When we look at our hardships through the lens of the gospel, we see this world is not our home. Our time of suffering on earth is short, but heaven's peace is eternal. So, despite the unrest in the world, we can still worship the Lord and sing "It Is Well with My Soul."

CLIMB THE MOUNTAIN
SCENE 6

With every painful step, I kept my eyes fixed on Jesus and the vision to reach the glorious mountaintop. Maintaining the vision of the summit in front of me helped me to faithfully persevere. One faithful step in front of the other helped me move forward ever so slowly in the right direction. As the vertical climb became much steeper and slower, I felt exhaustion setting into my body. Just then, I rounded the bend in the pathway and saw a sight that took my breath away. I wanted to belt out a high-pitched hallelujah chorus right then! A kind soul had built a tree log ladder with a railing to steady the ascent. It was perfect for giving relief to weary hikers like me at the most vertical part of the entire climb. It was such a morale booster to have help come unexpectedly out of nowhere to raise me up for the last part of the journey. It felt like a strong hand had just reached down and helped me at my point of greatest need.

It reminded me of another time when I was feeling particularly brokenhearted. While I was praying, the Lord reached down and lifted me out of the pit of despair and restored my hope. God's timing was perfect because while I was crying out to God to *do* something, I received a phone call from a dear friend who offered to fly me out to Colorado for a visit. At that very moment, it felt like the strong hand of God working through my dear friend to throw me a lifeline of encouragement. That week was such a beautiful time of friendship and laughter that came when I needed it most. It broke a long winter season of spiritual isolation and emotional drought. The divine intervention was undeniably God as He responded literally one minute after I cried out to Him. I wish I could say all my prayers are answered that quickly, but I treasure it in my heart as a remarkable example of God's provision and perfect timing.

I could tell by the tree line that I was close to the top, so I rallied all my strength and thanked Jesus as I limped up the last part of the ladder.

CHAPTER 6

RESTORING
PROMISES OF HOPE

And we boast in the hope of the glory of God. Not only so,
but we also glory in our sufferings, because we know that
suffering produces perseverance; perseverance, character;
and character, hope. And hope does not put us to shame,
because God's love has poured out into our hearts through
the Holy Spirit, who has been given to us.

Romans 5:2–5 NIV

Carry Me

After sobbing on my bed for at least a half an hour, I cried out aloud in prayer, "Lord, it has been such a long, hard journey of brokenness, and I don't know if I have the strength to go on much further. My grief is overwhelming. I can't do this anymore, and I'm begging you to please carry me." Instantly, I recalled a visual image of an old-fashioned Adirondack pack basket that was adapted by our early settlers from Native Americans.

The Adirondack pack basket existed long before our modern hiking backpack, and it was secure enough to carry small children, fishing gear, and camping items. People in the Adirondacks would create a pack basket by weaving together strips of soft black ash tree and adding adjustable leather straps to carry it on their shoulders. The basket was surprisingly strong and secure.

With tearstained cheeks, I visualized resting my hurting head on Jesus's shoulder, and He gently placed His hand on my head with loving reassurance. *My beloved daughter, I will carry you, and we will reach the summit together. I will be your comforter, your healer, and your guide.* The Lord tells us in Psalm 139:3–6, "You chart the path ahead of me and you tell me where to stop and rest. Every moment you know where I am. You know what I'm going to say even before I say it, Lord. You both precede and follow me. You place your hand of blessing on my head. Such knowledge is too wonderful for me, too great for me to know!"

After placing me in His pack basket, God whispered these tender words to me, *I will carry you as we climb the steep mountain and go through the wilderness valleys, and I will protect you during the darkest hours. I will go before you and guide you every step of the way through this perilous pathway. Don't give up hope, my child, I love you, and I promise to redeem your brokenness for a purpose that will amaze you.*

Beautifully Broken

The Holy Spirit can turn our broken mess into His redemptive mosaic masterpiece. "Some of us would never have looked up had we not hit bottom."[1] When our world shatters into a million pieces all around us, there is still hope. Our Lord specializes in restoration and He carefully collects all the broken pieces of our lives and assembles us back together in greater ways than we could ever dare to hope or imagine.

In brokenness we begin to recognize that we bring nothing to God that is worthy or righteous. Nowhere in Scripture does it say we must fix all the broken pieces of our lives before we come to God. We come to Him wearing our ragged robes of sin, baggage that is far too heavy for us to carry, tearstained faces, swollen eyes, and dirty hands. But as we come to our loving Abba

God carefully collects all the broken pieces of our lives and assembles us back together in greater ways than we could ever dare to hope or imagine.

Father, He smiles with His kind eyes and warmly embraces us in His arms—just as we are.

Our Abba Father then sheds tears of joy and showers us with kisses, saying, *Welcome home, child; you are dearly loved here.* He pulls away only for a moment to look deep in our eyes to tell us He is going to give us Christ's royal robes of righteousness to wear and remove our ragged clothes of sin. God will give us a spiritual inheritance, which includes a change of identity and a new purpose. Isaiah 61:3 (NLT) says, "He will give a crown of beauty for ashes, a joyous blessing instead of mourning, festive praise instead of despair. In their righteousness, they will be like great oaks that the Lord has planted for His own glory." Beautiful words.

"Before the acorn can bring forth the oak, it must become itself a wreck. No plant ever came from anything but a wrecked seed."[2] We are beautifully broken when we have been crushed for the divine purpose of spiritual growth. It is often through the cracks of a broken heart that the Holy Spirit can realign our soul and plant the

> *We are beautifully broken when we have been crushed for the divine purpose of spiritual growth.*

gospel message. "Jesus is trying to get us to understand a key dynamic principle. When we give up our tight grasp on our own life, we discover life as it was meant to be lived."[3] My friend, we can rest in the hopeful promise that the Lord will give us beauty for our ashes too.

Brokenness is not a onetime event, as some Christians might think. It is a continual sanctification growing process. The pruning knife cuts deep but clears away dead branches that will never produce anything. God's pruning knife is also used to cut back good fruit in our lives to produce even greater fruitfulness in the years to come. "Growth in godly character is not only progressive and always unfinished, it is absolutely necessary for spiritual survival. If we are not growing in godly character, we are regressing; in the spiritual life we never stand still."[4]

Viewing our brokenness as a necessary part of our spiritual growth gives us hope during the refining process. "Brokenness is God's requirement for maximum usefulness."[5] He wants our brokenness to propel us into a deeper relationship with Christ. Brokenness is the first step to rebuilding our self-worth based on Christ's merit and not our own. "Don't kick against your loving Father's refining process. He is allowing your circumstances to chip away all your dependence on your own flesh and instead opt for your identity in Christ."[6]

John 3:30 (ESV) says, "He must increase, but I must decrease." This biblical truth is in direct opposition to the world's ways of personal empowerment and self-improvement theories. Required brokenness is a key part of the restoration journey toward developing a Christ-centered character.

Coming to Jesus beautifully broken gets us off our "high horse" and allows us to humbly kneel before the cross next to our brothers and sisters. The posture of authentic humility helps us recognize that we all need our Savior to rescue us. "Humility gladly submits to God's rightful place as Lord. It produces a right spirit toward others and a grateful sense of submission to God's providing work on our behalf."[7] The Holy Spirit can help us deconstruct our mindset that is deeply rooted in self, consisting of our own righteousness, perfectionism, and successes. "The preoccupation with self is the enemy of humility."[8]

Brokenness is the first step to rebuilding our self-worth based on Christ's merit and not our own.

Only then will we realize that all "our works are like filthy rags" (Isaiah 64:6), and we bring nothing to the table. The scales will fall from our eyes so we can see with clarity that the Christian life is not about "me" at all. "Stubbornness and self-love give way to beauty in one who has been broken by God."[9] The overflowing work of the Spirit transforms our hearts, restores our hope, and helps us to become others-focused. Be encouraged, my friends. This is not something that is possible to do in our feeble human strength and willpower. God will do it for us. "'Not by might nor by power, but by my Spirit,' says the Lord Almighty" (Zechariah 4:6 NIV). As we kneel in prayer before the Lord in humility and brokenness, He promises to raise us up to be more than we could ever be.

> *The Holy Spirit can help us deconstruct our mindset that is deeply rooted in self, consisting of our own righteousness, perfectionism, and successes.*

Healing Presence

Who wouldn't want to see one of the Seven Wonders of the World? My church travel group had just left the stunning treasury building in Petra, Jordan, when we learned that there was a carved stone monastery at the top of the mountain. Petra is often called the "Rose City" because of the unique rose-colored rock from which the treasury building and monastery are carved.

I debated whether I should climb the mountain because I had been suffering for months from an abdominal ailment accompanied by unpredictable searing pain. The vertical incline was very steep, but there were stone steps carved into the mountain which guided us to the monastery. Let me tell you; it was a StairMaster on steroids. I decided to go for it and trust that God would sustain me.

It seemed like hours passed before I realized that my fears were causing me to miss the beauty of God's creation. As I reached a good stopping point on the mountain ledge, I hunched over to catch my breath. When I stood up and looked out at the horizon, I was overwhelmed by the stunning beauty of the plethora of mountain peaks and jagged rock formations and the magnificent view all around me. The Lord whispered in my spirit and said, *When you are so focused on your own pain, you miss all the beauty that I have created for you to enjoy.* Immediately, I was humbled with conviction, and I prayed, "Abba Father, please

> *As we kneel in prayer before the Lord in humility and brokenness, He promises to raise us up to be more than we could ever be.*

forgive me. Help me to look up and see that You are with me." To persevere, I needed to focus on my healer instead of my pain.

It was so exhilarating to finally reach the summit and see the rose-colored monastery glistening in the sunshine. Oddly, there was a vendor there to greet the tourists with refreshing apple tea. I laughed out loud. Can you imagine hiking this trek daily with a backpack full of apple tea supplies? I wandered away from the rest of the group so I could quietly sip my tea and soak in the panoramic mountain view. As I prayed with my eyes wide open, tears came down my cheeks as my heart swelled with hopeful gratitude. I whispered, "Thank you, Lord, for your healing presence." My hope was restored in that moment.

"Beauty brings us into places of healing, as well as into God's presence."[10] I gazed upon the rose-colored desert mountains as far as the eye could see and experienced God's majesty in the mountains. He enabled me to physically persevere and trust Him one stone step at a time. Even though the air was dry on the desert mountain, my soul overflowed with refreshing streams of living water. As I reflect on my mountain trek, it was clear that my attitude shift directly correlated with a renewed altitude perspective.

Attitude Shift

"God, why aren't you answering my prayers?" I cried out to God in frustration while I prayed on the screened-in porch at Lake Titus. I was being brutally honest about my discouragement. Suddenly, a miraculous shift of attitude occurred, and I was surprised by the words that came out of my mouth in prayer. Instead of asking God to remove the trial, I asked Him to increase my faith so I could persevere. Simultaneously, when the Holy Spirit changed my attitude, He also strengthened my innermost being and filled me with renewed hope. My friends, as Beth Moore said, "Make no mistake, it is intimacy with God when you are willing to wrestle something out with Him."[11]

The attitude shift helped me to feel lighter and more hopeful that the Lord had been working behind the scenes the entire time. I realized that "sometimes there are no easy answers, but His promises remain true."[12] One of God's hope-filled promises I rely on often is from Romans 8:28 (NIV): "And we know that in all things God works for the good of those who love him, who have been called according to his purpose." This doesn't mean that everything that has happened to us is good, but we can have faith that God will redeem it *for* our good and His glory.

We have a critical attitude choice between doubt and faith when we are faced with trials. "Doubt sees the obstacles; faith sees the opportunities."[13] The quickest way to succumb to despair is by doubting that God is going to work out your difficult situation. Please stop doubting! "God has not given us hundreds of promises simply for us to read and enjoy. God has given us His promises so we might boldly declare them to bring us victory, health, hope, and abundant life."[14]

My friend, hold on to the promise in the book of James; the Lord will grow your faith through it.

> Consider it all joy, my brothers and sisters, when you encounter various trials, knowing that the testing of your faith produces endurance. And let endurance have its perfect result, so that you may be perfect and complete, lacking in nothing. But if any of you lacks wisdom, let him ask of God, who gives to all generously and without reproach, and it will be given to him. But he *must ask in faith without any doubting,* for the one who doubts is like the surf of the sea, driven and tossed by the wind. For that person ought not to expect that he will receive anything from the Lord, being a double-minded man, unstable in all his ways.
>
> Blessed is a man who perseveres under trial; for once he has been approved, he will receive the crown of life which the Lord has promised to those who love Him." (James 1:2–8, 12 NASB, emphasis mine)

Doubting is a dangerous attitude in a personal storm because it causes our emotions to be tossed around like a sailboat without a centerboard. Shortly after my dad had acquired a seventeen-foot O'Day sailboat, our family headed out to a nearby lake. I was not with the family during this outing, but the hilarious story has become a family favorite that has been retold for decades.

My dad thought he didn't need any sailing lessons because he was certain he could just figure it out. After all, how hard can sailing be? Well, my family didn't listen to the small-craft weather warning and didn't think twice about it even as boaters were coming to shore in a mass exodus. My dad, mom, brother, and his wife were excited to set sail for the day. After all, the wind and waves make for a great sailing day, right? Wrong! They forgot to put the centerboard down so the boat bobbed up and down out of control in the storm. When my sister-in-law tried to fix the jib, the boom swung around and knocked her right off the boat into the water. Dad reached out and hoisted her back into the boat with one arm. This was the turning point when they decided to bring the sailboat to shore.

During this time, Mom was having a low-protein moment, and she gripped a tuna fish sandwich with both hands and began chomping it down like it was her last meal. She explained later that she wanted to make sure she had enough protein to give her strength if she needed to swim to shore. We still laugh out loud about the funny family sailing story to this day. It is amazing to see how the absence of a small wooden centerboard to stabilize the boat could cause total chaos on the water.

The same is true for us; our faith needs to remain centered in the hope we have in Christ—especially when we are in the middle of a personal storm. When times are tough, we may forget to put our centerboard down and set out on our own with disastrous results. Or, we can slow down, put our centerboard down into the truth of God's Word, which will keep us from capsizing. This is especially critical when you can't see God's promises coming to pass.

"Given the choice of viewing life through the rose-colored glasses of hope rather than the dark blinders of sadness, anger, and worry, wouldn't it be far better to assume you'll find a foothold amid the chaos? After all, even if you go under, won't you have enjoyed the swim all the more if you sustain hope until the end rather than sinking into despair?"[15]

Abraham remained steadfast in his faith despite how his circumstances appeared. "Even when there was no reason for hope, Abraham kept hoping—believing that he would become the father of many nations" (Romans 4:18). After such a long time of waiting for God's promises to unfold, Abraham easily could have given up hope. I wonder if Abraham ever went out at night to look at the stars in the heavens to remind himself of what God had promised him in Genesis 15:5 (NASB): "Now look toward the heavens, and count the stars, if you are able to count them. And He said to him, 'So shall your descendants be.'" Abraham trusted in God's faithfulness and believed His promises.

We, too, can meditate on God's promises in His Word for renewed hope which will sustain us during times of unanswered prayer. "Keep dreaming the dream that God has put into your heart."[16] My friends, never lose sight of the truth that God is faithful.

Faithfulness in the Desert

It was a beautiful night in Israel, and the sun was setting with brilliant colors of coral and magenta across the sky. Our jeep bounced across the Wadi Rum sand dunes while we sang worship songs at the top of our lungs. Amid the laughter and smiles, our jeep suddenly came to a screeching halt. Stepping out of the jeep onto the coarse, bright red sand, it appeared as though we had just landed on Mars. We made our way toward a mountain with a sizable crack in the base, which opened into a larger cave. Our guide led us deep inside the cave and showed us ancient drawings and writings on the wall that were over two thousand years old. Those drawings might have been from the Israelites wandering around the desert after their exodus from Egypt. I was thrilled to see ancient artwork and wondered about the artists who drew them.

After our cave exploration, we drove to a Bedouin tent in the middle of the desert for a traditional dinner. It was a large tent with Turkish rugs scattered on the ground to create a comfortable dining space. On our way into the tent, we passed by our dinner on display which consisted of several chickens and a lamb. Our hosts cooked the animals in the traditional way of slow cooking for hours over coals buried in a sand pit. While we waited to eat dinner, our male hosts were beckoning us to dance with them as the Turkish music blared in the background. They were dressed in Bedouin attire, gathering us together to dance around a circle, crossing our feet as we danced under the open sky filled with stars. The moon was full that night, and the stars filled the heavens. I thought about Abraham's promise.

Although the dinner was festive, my mind kept wandering back to the insightful teaching earlier that day. Pastor Jackson Crum told us, "The wilderness is often a time where God shows His faithfulness." When the Israelites were in the wilderness for forty years, it was an opportunity to grow in character, courage, and greater dependence on God. He went on to say that when we go through a spiritual or emotional desert season in life, God never forgets about us or puts us aside. We may lose sight of God's care and provision when we think God has forgotten us, but He is there nonetheless. Pastor Jackson challenged us with a great question, "How can we use our desert seasons to grow us in our faith?"[17]

His comments resonated with me deeply, and I reflected on my own desert times. I thought about Anne Lamott's quote, "Courage is fear that has said its prayers."[18] We all have pivotal life-changing choices to make to be fearful or courageous. "Having courage for the long-haul means embracing God's love in the face of unrelenting difficulty."[19] We can remain fearfully stuck in the barren desert or courageously move into the fertile promised land with the Lord's help. The choice is yours—just ask Him.

Master Gardener

A resilient faith is like a strong oak tree with deep roots that remains steadfast even during the fiercest storms. "Then Christ will make his home in your hearts as you trust him. Your roots will grow down into God's love and keep you strong" (Ephesians 3:17 NLT). Our Lord is a Master Gardener, and He has a spectacular kingdom plan for His magnificent garden. You might be wondering, *What is it like to be part of the Kingdom of God?* "The Kingdom of God is a Kingdom of limitless power, ceaseless joy, and unending peace. It is a Kingdom of righteousness, a Kingdom of love, and a Kingdom of right relationships."[20] I long to be part of this kind of kingdom garden here on earth. When I think about God's garden in heaven, I visualize a garden full of Adirondack wildflowers.

In the Adirondacks, open fields are filled with an assortment of wildflowers, such as mini-daisies, pink foxgloves, Queen Anne's lace, blue bells, yellow goldenrod, white trillium, blue forget-me-nots, and purple violets. Adirondack wildflowers are irregular in shape and size, and they sprout up in the most unexpected places. These wildflowers live up to their names. They will never have the mass-produced look of perfection. Instead, they carry their organic free spirit as they sway to the gentle music of the mountain breezes in the open countryside. They are surprisingly resilient, too, thriving despite the harsh weather of the North Country. Each blossom is designed with imperfect wild elegance.

As followers of Christ, we are also imperfect and slightly wild like the Adirondack wildflowers. Sadly, we often try to plant the seeds of our own plans and ask God to bless them with a harvest. When we ask the Lord to grow our faith, our Master Gardener is faithful to break up the hard soil and pull out the weeds that have prevented our faith from blossoming. "Faith recognizes that God is in control, not man. Faith does it God's way, in God's timing—according to His good pleasure. Faith does not take life into its own hands, but in respect and trust, places it in God's."[21] Pulling out the destructive deep roots of disillusionment is part of the preparation process to restoring our hope.

Is the Master Gardener pulling out the weeds in your carefully planned garden right now? Are you carrying the burden of a broken friendship? Are you going through a divorce? Have you been overlooked for a promotion? Did you get laid off? Have you been battling with a terminal illness? Are you reeling from the death of a loved one?

Are you struggling with an estranged family relationship? God understands how fragile you feel. Proverbs 13:12 (NLT) reminds us, "Hope deferred makes the heart sick, but a dream fulfilled is a tree of life." It is time to stop allowing the weeds of our broken dreams to crowd out our future hope.

We cannot change our past, but we can make better choices for a healthier present and future. "Pulling weeds and planting seeds. That's the story of life. We are individual lots on which either weeds of selfishness or fruit of the Holy Spirit grows and flourishes."[22] The Lord has graciously pulled out the weeds in my life, helped me let go of deep-rooted injustices, and planted new kingdom-centered dreams in my heart.

Letting Go

John Maxwell said, "Do you know how to die victoriously? Quit keeping score of the injustices that have happened to you." It is true that when we are confronted with the death of our loved ones, our priorities change. An eternal focus helps us to tear down the walls of injustices and place our trust in our loving Savior, whose throne is built on justice and righteousness. "No cruelty, no crime, no injustice escapes the attention of God."[23] God sees . . . and God knows.

As I was driving back through Saranac Lake on my way home to Connecticut, I realized that I have more work to do on letting go. Unresolved life disappointments can easily become blocks of ice with one stacked on top of the other until we have built an ice castle of hopelessness.

The Saranac Lake Winter Carnival began in the 1800s and is the longest running winter carnival in the Northeast. The iconic symbol of the winter festivities is a massive palace built entirely out of ice blocks that were cut out of the lake.

Every February the little town of Saranac Lake, New York, is ablaze with colorful ski sweaters, rosy cheeks, and friendly smiles. The winter parade is a way to break up the isolating gloomy winters, which can get down to twenty degrees below zero. The Winter Carnival celebration includes many social and sporting events and fireworks over the grand ice palace on Lake Flower. The winter sports include "snowflake volleyball" and "snowshoe softball." Can you imagine?

In the 1870s, a doctor named Edward Trudeau came to the Adirondacks to die from tuberculosis. In a miraculous way, the Adirondack fresh mountain air instead brought healing and restoration to Dr. Trudeau. With Dr. Trudeau's renewed sense of energy and vitality, he opened the first "Cure Cottage Sanatorium" in Saranac Lake to treat people suffering from tuberculosis. Word got out quickly, and tuberculosis patients flocked to the Adirondacks from New York City and all around the country. Residents of Saranac began building second-story porches and taking in tuberculosis patients to reside with them. It is common to see old photos with women in fur coats sitting outside on rocking chairs in the dead of winter to breathe in the fresh air.

Inhaling the fresh Adirondack air slowed the TB bacteria from spreading throughout their lungs. In a similar way, exhaling the injustices and letting go and inhaling God's promises, can stop further damage of the sin bacteria that decays our soul. If we do not view our suffering through the lens of the gospel, then our dreams deferred can solidify into a frozen, hard heart. It is not the way God wants us to live. The Lord's promises are filled with both present and eternal hope that can thaw out even the coldest of hearts.

Eternal Hope

The depth of Christ's love and mercy is greater than we will ever know this side of heaven. We can trust the one with the nail-pierced hands because He was willing to take our place. "In Jesus Christ, God experienced the greatest depth of pain. Therefore, though Christianity does not provide the reason for each experience of pain, it provides deep resources for actually facing suffering with hope and courage rather than bitterness and despair."[24] Christ died on our behalf so that we could have eternal hope.

"A season of suffering is a small price to pay for a clear view of God."[25] The apostle Paul knew this well. Paul suffered tremendously with a constant thorn in the flesh, a messenger from Satan to keep him from exalting himself. Three times, Paul pleaded for the torment to be taken away from him. God said, "My grace is sufficient for you, for my power is made perfect in weakness." What was Paul's response? He said, "Therefore, I will boast all the more gladly about my weaknesses, so that Christ's power may rest on me. That is why for Christ's sake, I am content in weaknesses, insults, in hardships, in persecutions, and calamities. For when I am weak, then I am strong" (2 Corinthians 12:8–10 ESV). Paul focused on eternal hope and believed God's promise for sustaining strength, and so can we.

Every person who is going to be a mighty instrument in God's hands will endure persecution and suffering here on this earth. In fact, this is one of God's promises, though we wish it was not. Suffering can make us bitter or better people. Warren Wiersbe says,

> Satan wants to use suffering to tear us down, but God can use suffering to build us up and equip us to serve him better. However, keep in mind that suffering does not automatically equip the saint. Sad to say, some Christians have gone through trials and have come out of the fiery furnace burned and bitter instead of purified and perfected. It is only when we depend on the grace of "God of all grace" that the furnace does its equipping work.[26]

The greatest spiritual growth and character refinement occurs on the road of suffering. God promises that when we are experiencing our weakest moments, God's glory will shine brightly through us to a watching world. "God does not want us to simply forget the pain of the past. He wants us to be fruitful in the land of our suffering! Use it for good. Minister to others. Plant seeds of hope."[27]

Suffering will never be the end of our story because we have faith and eternal hope in the One who has redeemed us. This is good news worth sharing to a broken world! Now go forth and bless others locally and globally with the hope you have been given in Christ.

Life Lessons Learned

The Lord has reassured me with His promises of hope throughout many adventures from the Adirondack wilderness to the desert mountains in Petra. From ice castles to gardens, He has metaphorically shown me how to let go of broken dreams and embrace His master kingdom plan, which is far greater than we could ever imagine or hope for.

A critical aspect of moving forward is to let your faith be bigger than your fear. "I am leaving you with a gift—peace of mind and heart. And the peace I give is a gift the world cannot give. So don't be troubled or afraid" (John 14:27 NLT). Many Christians have experienced a desert or wilderness season when God seems quiet. Even strong believers, such as Martin Luther, Charles Spurgeon, and Mother Theresa struggled with dark-night-of-the-soul experiences, but they kept believing, trusting, and moving forward in God's strength.

I, too, have had seasons when it has been hard to understand why God has allowed certain things to happen in my life. However, I discovered when I look upward and outward, instead of at my own world of disappointment, I see that God is still mightily at work all around me. Focusing on my healer more than my wounds allows my trust muscles to develop into strong faith muscles. God's promises of hope strengthen our faith muscles, which produces the stamina to persevere and climb the mountain before us.

When we doubt God less and start trusting Him more, we will begin to see renewed hope birthed in our souls. Brokenness is not the end of our story; it is a critical part of the ongoing sanctification process. It is a catalyst for spiritual growth and new direction, and it fosters a renewed perspective on what is truly important in life. After all, a mosaic masterpiece requires broken pieces. We must first become broken before we can be beautiful in our Savior's eyes.

Being refreshed by the promises in the Word of God heals our hearts and minds and renews our hope. "For whatever was written in former days was written for our instruction, that through endurance and through the encouragement of the Scriptures, we might have hope" (Romans 15:4 ESV). I have personally found that immersing myself in the Word of God and allowing His promises to wash over me renews my thinking. His promises are like an oasis of hope in the middle of a wilderness experience. The Lord has redeemed and blessed us so that we can bring His message of hope to a broken world.

Hoping in the glory of God while suffering refines our character, teaches us how to worship through the pain, and enables us to persevere when we want to quit. Trust me; when you are at your lowest point, the Lord will either carry you or throw you a lifeline of encouragement.

There is hope after our shattered dreams, and God will plant a new dream in your heart that will glorify Him. Are you beginning to see a new dream rise from the ashes of your life? The Lord can bring beauty from ashes and make broken things beautiful again.

CLIMB THE MOUNTAIN
SCENE 7

Streams of sunlight pierced through the darkness of the forest, and my pulse began to race. I could barely contain my excitement as I finally approached the clearing at the summit of Elephant's Head. I ignored my throbbing foot and hiked faster out of sheer adrenaline coursing through my veins. A mixture of delight and relief welled up in my eyes, tears flowing down my cheeks as I looked down at Lake Titus. I rested on a fallen log to take the weight off my foot and prayed.

"Thank you, Jesus, for giving me the strength to press on and persevere through the pain of my injury so I could experience your faithfulness and see a glimpse of Your glorious splendor at the summit." When I opened my eyes and looked around, I noticed someone who climbed the mountain before me had been inspired to carve the word *SPLENDOR* in capital letters on a nearby tree. Indeed, this glorious view of Lake Titus is a glimpse of God's splendor in the Adirondack Mountains.

From my vantage point, I could see the entire circumference of Lake Titus, which reminded me of the side profile of a foot. A smile spread across my face as I located our family camp at the highest point of the arch of the Lake Titus foot. How ironic that I injured my foot while climbing this mountain only to look down at a lake in the shape of a foot. Perhaps the image was to remind me that I need to slow down, trust God, and walk by faith. God is faithful, and I know with absolute confidence that whatever new mountain I faced in the future, He would give me the faith to climb it. He will be right there beside me.

Unexpectedly, a cool, refreshing wind covered me with the sweet fragrance of the cedars and pines nearby. The sunlight was bright, white-hot, and it took a while for my eyes to adjust. I closed my eyes and reflected on God's faithfulness. "We can learn the purpose of God as we fill ourselves with His Word and then look to Him for direction with a surrendered heart."[1] With God's direction, He has helped me overcome impossible situations and taught me how to trust Him with the process. For me, experiencing hardships has fostered a deeper dependency on the Holy Spirit and a greater urgency to share the hope and healing that is available in Christ.

The higher we climb, the greater our perspective. At the summit, I was surprised by the number of other mountains and bogs visible in the distance. Similarly, in the thick of the forest (or our personal crisis), it can be difficult to delineate between the trees and the forest as it all blurs together. Only when we ask Jesus to open our eyes to see our circumstances from His gospel perspective does the redemptive trail map make sense.

If we want the Lord to use our hardships for His glory, then we need to be willing to be transparent with others. "What is needed today is not a new gospel, but live men and women who can re-state the Gospel of the Son of God in terms that will reach the very heart of our problems."[2] When we authentically share the good news from a place of compassion and understanding, we can be instruments of Christ's hope to others in their hopeless situations.

The views from the mountaintop evoked a mixture of joy and relief, which made the climb entirely worth it. I am grateful that the Lord gave me the strength to persevere through the pain and press upward. It certainly is a metaphor for life, isn't it? I pulled out the crumbled Scripture card that filled me with hope along the hiking journey: "Jesus looked at them and said, 'With man this is impossible, but with God all things are possible'" (Matthew 19:26 NIV).

Thank you, Lord, for filling me afresh with the Holy Spirit's strength and giving me the faith to climb this mountain. Praise you,

Lord, for teaching me valuable life lessons over the many years and for turning my trials into triumphs for your glory. Amen.

CHAPTER 7

REACHING THE SUMMIT OF REDEMPTION

*And the God of all grace, who called you to his eternal glory
in Christ, after you have suffered a little while, will himself
restore you and make you strong, firm and steadfast.*

1 Peter 5:10 NIV

Trail Map

Following Christ's trail map involves walking by faith and not by sight. It can be difficult to understand God's ways, but we know that He is good, and we can trust Him. "When Jesus walked among humankind, there was a certain simplicity to being a disciple. Primarily it means to go with Him, in an attitude of study, obedience, and imitation."[1] The substance of our faith is tested when we are asked to give up everything and follow Him. Sometimes the simple request to follow Him can be the hardest to apply. Believe me, I understand.

Simply put, God's plans are bigger than my own. He called me back to Connecticut to care for several of my family members. It was difficult for me to leave my Chicago home, but through it all, I have grown spiritually in profound ways. The Lord has taken me deeper into a trust walk of faith as I experienced greater depths of surrender, patience, and long-suffering. You see, I had dreams for my life, but God had a much greater plan—one that I could never have imagined for myself. The Lord gave me the spiritual gift of faith when I accepted

Christ as my Savior and Lord as a seven-year-old, but each year, He continues to refine and strengthen my resolve. Over the years, my faith muscles have been stretched beyond comprehension as though I've been training for a Lake Placid Ironman in the Adirondack Mountains.

At times, the transition to Connecticut has seemed like a wilderness experience. However, there was a divine plan to peel away every idol in my heart so I could become deeply rooted in who I am in Christ. Unplugging from my busy life in Chicago allowed me to rest and recharge in the Holy Spirit's power so I could write this book. "Our main calling is to live in fellowship with Christ and to labor with Him in extending His kingdom."[2] I now see a glimpse of His larger trail map—a whole new ministry that He prepared for me long ago. "For we are God's masterpiece. He created us anew in Christ Jesus, so we can do the good things he planned for us long ago" (Ephesians 2:10 NLT). Writing and encouraging others about the goodness of God is both a passion and a ministry calling. I often wonder . . . would I have stepped into this new calling of writing for Him if I hadn't given up everything, picked up my cross and followed Christ to a destination unknown?

"Sometimes offering yourself as a vessel for the presence and work of God is costly."[3] The sacrificial cost of ministry requires giving up our own plans and giving our time and attention to those who need it. The ministry of availability requires slowing down, simplifying, listening to God's still, small voice, and a willingness to embrace divine appointments. "There is no higher calling or privilege in life to know Him and make Him known to others."[4] We are blessed to be a blessing to those around us. "Praise be to the God and Father of our Lord Jesus Christ, the Father of compassion and the God of all comfort, who comforts us in all our troubles, so that we can comfort those in any trouble with the comfort we ourselves receive from God" (2 Corinthians 1:3–4 NIV). We are comforted to be a comfort to the brokenhearted. Part of God's redemptive plan is to use us as His mountain guides to throw others a lifeline so they can navigate by faith the steep mountains above and deep valleys below.

Overcoming to Overflowing

The pancreatic cancer was winning the battle, and our time with my aunt was short. With my Bible in hand, I knelt on the floor next to the couch where Aunt Hazel was resting. I prayed and asked the Lord to give me wisdom on how best to encourage her in the Word as she was preparing to die.

Her body was weak, but her spirit was vibrantly alive in Christ. The Lord guided me to share with her a few verses beginning with Revelation 5:8–9 (ESV), "Golden bowls full of incense, which are the prayers of the saints. And they sang a new song, saying, worthy are you . . ." I reassured her that God had heard all her prayers, and they had been collected in golden bowls presented before Him as a sweet fragrance. The Lord heard every word, and He hears us now.

With a smile on my face, I recalled how the Lord had helped her overcome many personal mountains of hardship over the years. She nodded her head in agreement. I lovingly reminded her of the Scripture passage that everyone who "overcomes" will be clothed in white garments, and their name will be written in the book of life (Revelation 3:5).

My cousin, Julie, spoke up and said, "Did you know there are seven passages in Revelation that speak about overcoming?" And then Julie shared several Scripture verses that were meaningful to her. Together, we talked about how Christ warned us that we would suffer in this world, but God would help us overcome the suffering and promises to make all things new eternally.

"Our way to heaven lies through the wilderness of this world."[5] As we climb our mountains, we can rest in the hopeful promise about heaven.

> He will wipe away every tear from their eyes; and there will no longer be any death; there will no longer be any mourning, or crying, or pain; the first things have passed away. And He who sits on the throne said, "Behold, I am making all things new." And He said, "Write, for these words are faithful and true." Then He said to me, "It is

done! I am the Alpha and the Omega, the beginning and the end. I will give water to the one who thirsts from the spring of the water of life, without cost. The one who overcomes will inherit these things, and I will be his God and he will be My son." (Revelation 21:4–7 NASB)

Our tears on earth are temporary, but our joy in heaven is eternal. When times get rough, we can focus on the truth that the best is yet to come. "What is heaven, but to be with God, to dwell with Him, to realize that God is mine, and I am His?"[6] I long for that day when the Lord will wipe away my tears and make all things new again.

When we remember God's faithfulness through our wilderness seasons, He fills our hearts afresh with gratitude. I encouraged Aunt Hazel to silently name the relationships or events that were the hardest for her to overcome on this earth, the ones that had caused the most tears, pain, and grief. She closed her eyes and prayed as she recalled her steepest mountains. When she opened her eyes again, I read from Revelation 2:17 (NASB), "To the one who overcomes, I will give some of the hidden manna, and I will give him a white stone, and a new name written on the stone which no one knows except the one who receives it."

Aunt Hazel's eyes twinkled when I told her that her new name will declare her victory in Christ. I'm confident "we have a glorious future awaiting us beyond death's door."[7] Imagine the glorious reunion with so many loved ones who have gone before us. Aunt Hazel, I know you will be waiting on the heavenly shores to welcome me home someday. As we hugged goodbye, I told her I loved her, and I thanked her for her legacy of loving Jesus and blessing others with encouragement. He redeemed her heartbreak when she comforted others. I was filled with emotion as I prayed for the Lord to ease her suffering. I looked back one more time before I walked through the door, to capture her smiling face in my memory. I thought to myself, *Cancer may have temporarily won the battle, but Jesus won the eternal war at the cross.* Because of Christ's redemption, I know I will see her again in heaven.

I've often reflected on our last moments together and the passages we discussed in her living room. I decided to delve into the meaning of the Greek word for *overcome*, and what I discovered overwhelmed me with God's goodness. The range of meaning for the Greek word includes "to conquer, to come off victorious." The word *victorious* describes Christians who hold fast to their faith even unto death against the power of their foes and temptations and persecutions.

To overcome means to be victorious! If we remember whose we are, and whose we are, we will remain steadfast in our faith. "We live on a broken planet, fallen far from God's original intent. It takes effort to remember who we are, God's creation, and faith to imagine what we someday will be, God's triumph."[8] Our faith steps will lead us over the mountain of suffering to overflowing with God's grace like a mountain stream toward others. The Lord helped Aunt Hazel's faith to be eternally victorious in the heat of the cancer battle. My friends, I want to reassure you, in Christ's strength, you will experience freedom and victory, too.

Freedom and the Mother of Exiles

The Statue of Liberty's face is full of resolve with her head held upright, her powerful arm thrusting upward a torch with a flame in the air, and her stance evoking a cry of victory. Her feet are set in a forward motion as the shackles are being broken off, enabling her to step forward in freedom. The ripples of her dress cascade down with graceful movement. Lady Liberty is truly an exquisite work of art, and she carries so much symbolism in her presence and posture. It is no wonder they call her the Mother of Exiles as her face turns toward the weary travelers to welcome them to the city of possibilities. With the New York skyline looming behind her, her lighted torch is a welcome sight to those who flee their countries in search of freedom, who want to start a new life for themselves and their families.

Emma Lazarus (1849–1887) wrote the poem "The New Colossus" as a beacon of hope for people coming to America. A phrase that struck a chord in me was "Give me your tired, your poor, your huddled masses yearning to breathe free." Yes, freedom is a universal desire within each person around the world. So many people have looked to Lady Liberty to fulfill their yearning for freedom, yet only Jesus can truly fulfill the deepest longing for freedom in our hearts. "Christ's death was not a case of heroism; it was a case of redemption."[9] Because of Christ's work of redemption on the cross, we have been set free to live for Christ.

While I toured the museum inside the Statue of Liberty, I thoughtfully listened to the audio of the voices of immigrants. Their emotions were palpable as I listened to men and women recall their long voyage across the stormy sea to come to America. Many of them left their countries in search of dreams in the land of freedom. They were willing to sacrifice everything to seek and find it. They left generations of history and culture behind. Their lives were stuffed into tiny suitcases with a burning hope in their hearts for a new beginning. One man explained, "She was a beautiful sight after a miserable crossing that September. She held such promise for us all with her arm flung high, the torch lighting the way—opening a new world to those who would accept the challenge." Another unnamed female voice expressed, "Tears of joy streamed down my face as we passed by the Statue of Liberty." Lady Liberty represented the priceless word *freedom* to the immigrants who desired to have a better life for themselves and their families in this new world of possibilities.

"Where the Spirit of the Lord is, there is liberty" (2 Corinthians 3:17 NASB). When we turn our lives over to Christ and let go of the things of the past, we, too, can experience the greatest kind of freedom. We have been freed to serve Christ. "The opposite of a slave is not a free man. It's a worshipper. The one who is most free is the one who turns the work of his hands into a sacrament, into an offering. All he makes and all he does are gifts from God, through God, and to God."[10] As we embrace our freedom in Christ, we enter into a world of possibilities where new dreams and opportunities are born. It is never too late, and we are never too old to begin again in God's economy.

Shortly after the tragedy that rocked the nation on 9/11, I went to Ground Zero over the Thanksgiving weekend. I saw the site of the World Trade Center disaster, and it truly was a sobering experience. As I looked at the heap of twisted metal, I was impacted by the enormity of the destruction. When one views heinous, human atrocity in person, it feels surreal. There was a pungent smell in the air, a combination of smoldering metal, toxic chemicals, and heaps of ashes. I stood in front of an old church near Ground Zero and faintly attempted to absorb the meaningful tribute to the people who lost their lives in the World Trade Center. White bed sheets were thrown over the wrought iron fence surrounding the little church. They were strewn with handwritten notes, photos of those who lost their lives, and big and small American flags. Flowers and white pillar candles illuminated the shrine on the ground.

As I scanned the many written messages, I was struck by how often God was mentioned as loved ones cried out to Him in prayer. Families and colleagues who had lost someone in the World Trade Center wrote messages of Christ's hope next to the photos of the deceased. I was struck by such a contrast between pain and faith as I looked at the twisted metal of Ground Zero just beyond the church.

There were many stories about people who were supposed to be in the World Trade Center building that morning, but thankfully were not, including one of my dearest friends. I was profoundly grateful that God spared her life. My heart was filled with compassion for the families who did lose someone in the catastrophic event, and I prayed for God to comfort them in their pain. Our nation grieved for the many who senselessly lost spouses, children, and friends that day. Their suffering was heard around the world.

Close to the ten-year anniversary of 9/11, I felt drawn to revisit the World Trade Center. A memorial was under construction that would honor those who had lost their lives on that infamous day that changed America. I walked around the two pools of continuously flowing fountains with the names of the deceased etched in granite around the perimeter. I learned on that visit that the plans were to rebuild six new skyscrapers, a museum, memorial site, and several other buildings to replace the Twin Towers. The architectural integrity of several buildings around the World Trade Center was greatly affected by the explosions, and they needed to be torn down and rebuilt as well. I thought, *Despite the great destruction, multiplication would occur.* This is a powerful spiritual metaphor. The same is true for us. By God's grace, our lives can be rebuilt in the face of tragic loss. The Lord redeems and returns to us far more than what the Enemy takes from us.

The Statue of Liberty became a symbol of resilience and hope for America after the 9/11 tragic event. Even though the Twin Towers were called her shoulders in the New York City skyline, Lady Liberty was still standing tall and continued to be a symbol of America remaining strong through the national crisis. As believers, anytime we are faced with a personal crisis, our hope lies with Christ's redeeming work on the cross. "The cost of redemption cannot be overstated. The wonders of grace cannot be overemphasized. Christ took the hell He didn't deserve so we could have the heaven we don't deserve."[11] Hebrews 13:14 says, "For this world is not our permanent home; we are looking forward to a home yet to come." We can have hope because we know our permanent home is in heaven. Jesus has prepared a room for us right now in eternity, and it will be filled with complete joy.

Soar on Eagle's Wings

The more we trust God with our circumstances, the higher He will lift us up. As we draw closer to the Lord, we can discern what is important in life and what is not. The Holy Spirit guides us to let go of life's disappointments. My friends, the weight of the world attempts to pin us down, but when the Holy Spirit sets us free with His gospel-centered perspective, we can soar high above the fray. I believe we were created to soar on eagle's wings.

Have you ever stopped and watched an eagle glide effortlessly on a thermal wind current in the open sky? Watching from my Adirondack chair on the dock, I was amazed the eagle I spotted did not flap its wings or exert any energy at all. It soared with its wings outstretched while being lifted by the wind higher toward the sun. I amused myself by personally relating to a ruby-throated hummingbird whose wings are beating faster than fifty-three times a second! Can you relate to the feeling of constant busyness? I know our hearts long to soar effortlessly, and the Holy Spirit shows us how we can. When we rest in the promises of God, the Holy Spirit will raise us up higher than the storm clouds below us, and we will begin to see God's redemptive perspective. "Strictly speaking, of course, not one of us deserves redemption. God owes us nothing, but He nevertheless offers His undeserved grace. Though we deserve damnation, He invites each of us to be redeemed."[12] The Lord has redeemed us so we can experience abundant life where we can soar high above the weight of the world.

My father, Gordon Carl Todd, loves the American eagle and the majesty, strength, and freedom it represents. He grew up in a small, rural community in upstate New York, joined the army, and saw the world while he served in the armed forces. Upon his return to New York, he attended Houghton College and later transferred to the business school at Syracuse University. He worked at the Travelers Insurance Company for nineteen years before taking the very brave step to start his own business at age forty-five. My dad lived the American dream, and his dedication drove him to be a good provider. I am grateful to my father for his sacrifice and the legacy of his hard work ethic, perseverance, and entrepreneurial spirit. While growing up, Dad would often tell my brother and me, "There is no such word as *can't* in the Todd household; you *can* do it; you just need to work harder." That was my dad's motto! Never give up!

My father's great love for Lake Titus and the Adirondacks is also a legacy that will be passed down for generations. Titus has been a place of laughter and fellowship as well as a healing place of rest and renewal for the entire family. My parents have been loving and supportive especially during the hard seasons of life. In God's redemptive fashion, I have returned the blessing as their primary caregiver for many years during their battles with cancer and other health issues. One day, while Dad was battling stage 4 cancer, he said to me, "Sharon, if I die tomorrow, I know where I am going, and I am ready." I could see his heart transformation and his peace with God. By God's grace and strength, he overcame the cancer and other health challenges that could have easily taken his life. We thank God for the miracle that Dad is still with us today.

Two of Dad's greatest joys on earth were his family and his summer camp. He had great anticipation of returning to Lake Titus, where his heart would soar above the mountaintops with the eagles. Dad's favorite verse is Isaiah 40:30–31 (NLT): "Even youths will become weak and tired, and young men will fall in exhaustion. But those who trust in the Lord will find new strength. They will soar high on wings like eagles. They will run and not grow weary; they will walk and not faint." What an incredible promise God has given us in this passage.

Ask yourself, if you die unexpectedly tomorrow, are you ready? Do you intimately know the *only* one who saves us, redeems us, and gives us eternal life? "For God so loved the world that He gave his one and only son, that whoever believes in him will not perish but have eternal life" (John 3:16 NIV). "There will be no second chance after death, the time to prepare is now."[13] The pathway to a gospel-centered faith is simple. Romans 10:9 (ESV) declares, "Because if you confess with your mouth that Jesus is Lord and believe in your heart that God raised him from the dead, you will be saved." If you take the step of faith today, you will have God's blessed assurance for tomorrow. "When we receive Christ as our Savior, we receive absolute assurance that we will spend eternity with God. That assurance gives us the hope and the courage to endure sorrow, disappointments, and dangerous, difficult times."[14] Won't you join me and soar on eagle's wings full of God's peace and blessings for today and assurance for tomorrow? Following Christ on a redemptive adventure of faith will bring unimaginable blessings.

Overcoming Doubt Brings Unexpected Blessings

My mind was half asleep and on autopilot when I dragged the kayak into the lake near the boathouse that morning. I unknowingly over-extended the placement of my foot just a little too far to the left of center. So, when I hoisted my body into the kayak, it completely flipped over, submerging me into the cold Adirondack lake. I was completely stunned—*What just happened?*

I looked down in disbelief until my kayak started making a gurgling noise as it began to sink. My adrenaline kicked into high gear, and I used all my upper-body strength to hoist the kayak out of the water, heaving the boat onto dry land. *Nothing like a morning polar bear dip when it is forty-five degrees out!* That freezing water wake-up call was better than a Starbucks double shot of espresso, but I don't recommend it.

Later that morning, I sat in my Adirondack chair with a hot cup of coffee in my hands and reflected on what had happened. As a writer, I thought about the metaphorical parallels between resigning from ministry and unexpectedly flipping my kayak. Both experiences were humbling, jarring, and completely drained me of joy! Looking back, I was on autopilot in my career when I experienced a huge wake-up call. After both experiences, where everything was turned upside down, I doubted myself and my abilities. I needed God's wisdom to help me move forward and not pull back. This was a critical juncture because "every decision has an outcome, and every path has a destination."[15] I desperately wanted to be in the center of God's will where I would experience the most joy.

A few weeks had gone by, and sunshine was streaming through the cracks of my bedroom window shades with the intensity of a French horn playing a rise-and-shine wake-up song. I rubbed my eyes and sat up, instantly knowing that this was the morning I should take the kayak out again.

After recalling the last cold dip in the lake, I had to psych myself up. It was colder out this time, so I grabbed my wool hat and gloves and ran down the front steps and walked briskly to the boathouse. I was determined that I was not going to let my last experience steal my joy. After all, why should I let one bad experience derail me from doing what I love to do? "Then I realized, joy is more than a feeling; it is a deep peace blended together with a solid hope that God has not left us. Joy is a delight in knowing there will be a better day. Can we have joy as our companion even when the road gets bumpy? Absolutely."[16] I made the decision to shake off the bad experience and embrace joy that morning.

While I dragged the boat out to the lake, I said a quick prayer asking God to help me keep the kayak steady. Unsure of my footing, I kept moving my foot to be certain I had the correct placement before hoisting in the rest of my body. I could not believe how much I doubted myself. I prayed one more time and then just went for it. I heaved my body inside the kayak and landed on the seat with a loud thud, and a huge smile spread across my face. *Yeah, I made it!* I started paddling and thought I would go for just a brief trip down the lake because it was freezing outside.

As I paddled on the lake, the Holy Spirit nudged me to go farther. My attitude was a little whiny, and I said, "Really, God? But I'm tired and I'm cold." I sensed He was going to show me something beautiful in nature, so I asked Him, "What are you going to show me, a blue heron? A beaver? Another wood duck? I've already seen those animals."

Even though I was a little annoyed, I kept paddling until I made it into the second forest-covered alcove. As I eased the boat toward the shoreline, I still didn't see anything spectacular. I waited in the alcove for a long time and was beginning to second-guess myself. Until finally, feeling disappointed, I resigned myself to turn my kayak around and head back home.

Suddenly, I heard a strange sound in the water. I looked but I couldn't see anything, and then I saw them out of the corner of my eye. There were several large animals the size of beavers in the water, but they didn't look or sound like them. They were very playful and diving under the waterline, always staying close to each other. They spotted me and were curious about the big yellow kayak and the weird-looking lady with a blue coat, brightly colored hat, and gloves. The animals had big whiskers and made a hissing noise; their heads came out of the water about twelve inches to look at me.

I was fascinated. *What amazing animals!* They bobbed their heads up and down, coming closer as if to say, *Hi, wanna play?* As they went back and forth several times, all I could do was thank God over and over, marveling at this awesome experience. I was still trying to figure out what kind of animals they were, but then I spotted a long, round tail (not flat) as one dove under the water. *Hmmm, they are definitely not beavers, I thought.* It wasn't until I got home that it fully registered in my brain that the wonderful, playful creatures were freshwater otters! I had never seen them before in the wild. God had totally knocked my socks off in a way that He knew would bring me great joy and delight.

Still in awe, I picked up my cell phone and saw that I had a voicemail from a dear friend who had left a message saying that she was praying that God would encourage me today by showing me in a fresh way how much He loved me. I checked the time on the phone and realized she had left the message at the exact time when I saw the otters. The Lord is in all of the details, and He leads us into new adventures beyond what we could ever imagine. When He speaks to us, we need to follow Him regardless of whether it makes sense to us or not.

What a redemptive reassurance it was to have overcome my doubt and replaced it with unexpected blessings. God's nature is one of redemption, and He wants to turn our doubts into joy. "Joy is a choice. It's a matter of attitude that stems from one's confidence in God—that He is at work, that He is in full control, that He is in the midst of whatever has happened, is happening and will happen. Either we fix our minds on that and determine to laugh again, or we wail and whine our way through life. We determine which way we will go."[17] Despite our life circumstances being turned upside down, He helps us overcome our fears, renews our joy, and fills us to overflowing with gratitude.

Overflowing with Gratitude

"The first great characteristic of the true Christian is always a sense of thankfulness and of gratitude to God."[18] Despite circumstances, overflowing with gratitude and joy is not dependent on the trial being over. "Joy is not the fruit of the 'favorable' circumstances. Rather, it's the outpouring of a contented heart."[19] We can embody the fruit of the Spirit *while* going through the trial. I know that it seems impossible to experience joyful gratitude when your heart has been torn to shreds, but we can still be thankful for Christ's sacrifice that blesses us for eternity. "For our present troubles are small and won't last very long. Yet they produce for us a glory that vastly outweighs them and will last forever!" (2 Corinthians 4:17 NLT).

God's love endures forever. "Trust God's love. His perfect love. Don't fear He will discover your past. He already has. Don't fear disappointing Him in the future. He can show you the chapter in which you will. With perfect knowledge of the past and perfect vision of the future, He loves you perfectly in spite of both."[20] Out of His great love for us, the Lord has promised to redeem our wilderness season and give us mountain springs where there once was dry land.

God delights in using broken people and redeeming their experiences for His glory. Someone who has overcome cancer can encourage others during their cancer battles. Someone who has weathered many storms in ministry can mentor someone else through ministry challenges. The very nature of our Lord is to redeem our cross stories. Our Sovereign Lord redeems all things. Christ died so that you and I can be made new again and bear spiritual fruit for the kingdom.

Pruned for Greater Fruitfulness

The fruit of a redeemed life changes from being inwardly fixated to being outwardly focused. The Holy Spirit produces the fruit of righteousness in us and through us when we share about Christ's redemptive work in our lives. Proverbs 11:30 (NIV) states, "The fruit of the righteous is a tree of life, and the one who is wise saves lives." The fruit of our salvation is shown in the way that we comfort others with Christ's words that build up and edify. Proverbs 15:4 (NIV) says, "The soothing tongue is a tree of life." Are our words bringing life, hope, and encouragement to others, or are our words all about our own suffering?

The fruit of our words should share wisdom from the Scriptures. Proverbs 3:18 says, "Wisdom is a tree of life to those who embrace her;

happy are those who hold her tightly." Are we sharing God's wisdom from His Word, or are we sharing empty worldly wisdom? Wisdom is often formed through the crucible of suffering. We can grow wiser if we cling to Christ to help us overcome the seasons of crisis.

"To him who overcomes, I will grant to eat from the tree of life, which is in the Paradise of God" (Revelation 2:7 NASB). In heaven, the fruit from the Tree of Life will be available in abundance. Revelation 22:2 (NASB) says, "On either side of the river was the tree of life, bearing twelve kinds of fruit, yielding its fruit every month; and the leaves of the tree were for the healing of the nations." The leaves from the Tree of Life will be used to heal the nations of their pain, sorrow, and incurable wounds.

While reading *Streams in the Desert*, a devotional, I came across a quote from Joseph Caryl that I must share with you. "God selects the best and most notable of His servants for the best and most notable afflictions, for those who have received the most grace from Him are able to endure the most afflictions. In fact, an affliction hits a believer never by chance but by God's divine direction. He does not haphazardly aim His arrows, for each one is on a special mission and touches only the heart for whom it is intended. It is not only the grace of God but also His glory that is revealed when a believer can stand and quietly endure an affliction."[21]

One day we will be totally healed when we are in Christ's glorious and righteous presence. "You don't know how the Lord will redeem your life from the pit, but you must trust by faith, that He will. Like the little boy who offered the loaves and the fish to the disciples without knowing how Jesus would use them, offer your circumstances to the Lord. He knows how to transform the worst of circumstances into miraculous healing."[22] Now, that hopeful message is good news worth sharing! When we share about what Christ has done for you and me, we cannot help but radiate contagious joy.

Moments of Joy

"Joy is for the journey, especially the most difficult parts of it, not just for the reflective moments after the storm."[23] In the beginning of my trekking journey, I felt a deep sadness like an incurable wound, but over time, the Lord healed my wounds and turned my grief into joy. God gave me a new community in Connecticut with a new purpose. I learned how His promises are true, that "those who plant in tears will harvest with shouts of joy" (Psalm 126:5 NLT). It hasn't been an easy trek, but the lessons learned along the path have been priceless.

When we are going through a time of grief, it is easy to focus our attention on ourselves, but that self-focus will only lead to dwelling on the wrong things. When we fix our eyes on Jesus and the promises in His Word, the Holy Spirit will refresh our hearts and minds and give us overflowing joy. Chuck Swindoll reminds us that, "Joy is a choice. It is a matter of attitude that stems from one's confidence in God—that He is at work, that He is in full control, that He is in the midst of whatever has happened, is happening and will happen. Either we fix our minds on that and determine to laugh again, or we wail and whine through life. We determine which way we will go."[24] Sometimes we need the Holy Spirit to redirect our focus and our thoughts.

My mother often shares pearls of godly wisdom at the perfect time. One particular morning, when I was discussing my writing on joy, she shared another pearl with me. She said that joy can be broken down into an acronym (J-O-Y) for changing our focus so we will experience true joy. First focus on Jesus; then focus on others; and only then, focus on yourself:

J = Jesus

O = Others

Y = Yourself

When we focus first on Christ, the rest of our perspective and priorities will come into proper alignment. "When Christ is the center of our lives, when His glory is our goal, when we refuse to be intimidated by life's obstacles, and when we live totally for Christ in obedience, we will find a joy that will carry us through the darkest of valleys."[25] This has been true for me. As I journaled about the joy in the journey of climbing the mountain, I realized it was the Lord's active presence that provided many moments of joy along the way. I wanted to share a few with you:

Joy in taking long walks and noticing the intricate beauty in nature

Joy in having time to reflect and write about God's goodness and grace

Joy in being still in God's presence on the dock at Lake Titus

Joy in the Ouch-Hallelujah moments of conviction and repentance

Joy in recognizing that our true Enemy is Satan and not people

Joy in creating a network of community care with my neighbors during the pandemic

Joy in studying God's Word and praying for each other in my women's small group

Joy in serving and caring for my elderly parents when they needed it most

Joy in traveling overseas and at home

Joy in making memories with my family that will last a lifetime.

Joy in doing the right thing, even when it hurts, and loving anyway

Joy in writing this book to help others climb the mountains before them

Joy in the freedom of letting go of past disappointments and broken dreams

Joy in experiencing new dreams fulfilled

Joy in forgiving the unforgivable

Joy in being victorious despite fierce opposition

Joy in growing through conflict resolution and grace

Joy in my redeemed identity in Christ

Joy in knowing that the battle is the Lord's, and He has already won the war

Joy in knowing the Lord is always with me in the valleys and on the mountain tops

Joy in believing God's promises in His Word

Joy in seeing my faith become stronger than my fears

Joy in seeing God's miraculous answers to prayer

Joy in God's amazing provision when I needed it most

Joy in seeing my faded scars but no longer feeling the pain

Joy in releasing idols and being given a new clean heart of worship

Joy in God's Word washing over me with His unfailing love

Joy from a fresh infilling of the Holy Spirit to accomplish the impossible

Joy in having time for the ministry of presence

Joy in unexpected divine appointments

Joy in surrendering my plans and following Christ

Joy in holding my newborn grandniece in my arms

Joy in surrendering to God's priorities above my own

Joy in moving past the boulders in life and being an overcomer

Joy in being blessed so that I can be a blessing to others

Joy in serving, giving, and living for the glory of God

Joy in moving from isolation to a loving community

Joy in reaping a great harvest of patience and perseverance

Joy in working unto the Lord and not for man's praise

Joy in creating opportunities for community and connection

Joy in my cup overflowing with gratitude and thanksgiving

Joy in living fully in the present while embracing hope for the future

Joy in soaking in the beauty of God's creation in the Adirondack wilderness

Joy in the journey of climbing the mountain and reaching the summit

Radiant joy comes from being in the presence of the Lord. You and I have the freedom to be in Christ's presence every time we open the Bible and read His living Word. If you find your joy waning and negativity overtaking your attitude, ask yourself, "How is my prayer life and time in the Word right now?" Always remember, our joy is a witness to a watching world. "Christians without joy are basically useless to the work of God. They will enter heaven when they die, but they will take no one with them. After all, who would want what they have?"[26] Authentic joy despite our circumstances can only come from Christ.

Life Lessons Learned

Even though it had been several months since arriving at our family camp at Lake Titus, it was still thrilling to rush down to the dock to see God's splendor revealed in the morning sunrise. God paints a brand-new canvas each morning, and His creative artistry is awe-inspiring. I leaned back into the cedar Adirondack chair, sipped my coffee, and smiled as I said, "Good morning, Jesus, I love you." I thought about how much I have treasured my time at Lake Titus to pray, seek God's face, and write this book. I have cherished the adventure and am filled with gratitude over the opportunity to write at my beloved camp in the Adirondack Mountains.

Just then, a golden sun peeked over the mountains and seemed to rest there for a few moments before it unveiled its glory. With the sun rays cascading down, the face of the lake transformed from a slate blue-gray color into golden tones caressing the ripples of the waters. The intensity of the sun was so brilliant that it hurt my eyes to gaze upon it. Instantly, I thought of God's righteousness, holiness, and power. One cannot fully take it in without being permanently altered. As much as I delighted in the beauty of the bright sunshine, I had no choice but to close my eyes and soak in the warmth of the intense heat while the light radiated around me. I whispered, "His righteousness will shine like the dawn," and I instantly felt reassured that God was going to redeem my circumstances better than I could ever have imagined. I prayed, "I trust you Lord. May you be glorified."

When we follow Jesus on an adventure, we will leave many things behind, but He promises to go with us and take us to incredible places we never dreamed of going. Throughout this hike that is our life, we grow more dependent upon the Holy Spirit's power as our endurance is tested. So many life lessons will surface as we climb the mountain—He has great things to teach us along the way. Christ shines His light on invisible snares so we don't get tangled up on the trail. He releases the heavy baggage in our backpacks and helps us to press on past the boulders that attempt to obstruct our calling. "When the Bible says that you have been redeemed, it means that you have been absolutely freed, fully released, and totally delivered from all that had you bound in the past." We are His new creations with a fresh start and a new purpose.

As our Adirondack guide, Jesus gives us trail markers to guide our path to new beginnings and provides support in unexpected ways. "He makes me as surefooted as a deer, enabling me to stand on mountain heights" (Psalm 18:33 NLT). When we experience discouragement, He showers us with comfort and refreshes us with His living water and promises of hope. He releases us from old names and false identities that tear us down, and He builds us back up in His identity. "It is easier to walk in triumph every day when we know that the condemnation is gone and we're free to live in victory."[27] We have been washed clean by the blood of the Lamb and given His righteousness.

Every experience has purpose. "Nothing can happen to a child of God outside the will of God."[28] Through every metaphorical ascent and decent on the trail of life, we must always keep our eyes focused on Jesus and trust with believing faith that "the best is yet to come. When we have the summit of heaven as our focus, we realize that this world is not our home. The passage in 2 Corinthians 4:17–18 (NLT) says, "For our present troubles are small and won't last very long. Yet they produce for us a glory that vastly outweighs them and will last forever! So we don't look at the troubles we can see now; rather we fix our eyes on the things that cannot be seen. For the things we can see now will soon be gone, but the things we cannot see will last forever." Our troubles on this earth are temporary and will soon fade away. God has uniquely designed each of us with spiritual gifts to be used for a special purpose and calling while we are here on earth. He wants us to worship Him despite our grief, become more like Christ through our hardships, and share the hope of the gospel to a broken world that desperately needs to know Jesus.

Your summit victory and radiant joy will encourage others to begin their own faith trek. Never lose sight of our spiritual summit. "We are more than conquers through Him who loved us" (Romans 8:37 NIV). Whatever new mountains we face in the future, we can be confident He will give us the faith to climb them.

Your faith journey continues with the Transformational Trek Study Guide downloaded from Sharon's website at www. SharonEleanorTodd.com. Questions and journaling reflections lead you on a spiritual hike to repurpose your pain for His glory and discover the God of new beginnings.

WOUNDED IDENTITY VS. REDEEMED
IDENTITY CHART

Wounded Identity	God's Promise	Redeemed Identity
1. Angry	Romans 5:1	I am at peace with God.
2. Lonely	John 15:15	I am Christ's friend.
3. Damaged	2 Corinthians 5:17	I am a new creation in Christ.
4. Weak	2 Corinthians 12:9	I am given Christ's power.
5. Empty	John 17:13	I am filled with Christ's joy.
6. Worthless	Ephesians 2:10	I am God's masterpiece.
7. Unclean	Acts 15:9	I have been purified by faith.
8. Orphaned	Ephesians 1:5	I was chosen for adoption.
9. Fearful	2 Timothy 1:7	I have been given power, love, and a sound mind.
10. Anxious	Philippians 4:6	I can replace my anxiety with prayer.
11. Condemned	Romans 8:1	I have been freed from condemnation.
12. Unholy	1 Corinthians 3:16	I am the temple of God.
13. Rejected	1 Peter 2:9	I am part of a chosen people, a royal priesthood.
14. Despair	Romans 15:13	I will abound in hope by the power of the Holy Spirit.
15. Sorrow	Psalm 30:5	I will have joy in the morning.
16. Rebellious	Ezekiel 36:25–27	I will have a new soft and obedient heart.
17. Powerless	Philippians 4:13	I can do all things through Christ who strengthens me.
18. Bondage	Romans 6:18	I am free by God's grace.
19. Old Nature	Romans 6:11	I have been given a new nature.
20. Defeated	Romans 8:37	I have overwhelming victory through Christ.
21. Unlovable	1 John 4:12	I am completely loved by God.

APPENDIX 2
VICTORY STRATEGIES: SPIRITUAL TACTICS, GEAR, AND WEAPONS
(Ephesians 6:10–20 and 2 Chronicles 20:1–30 NIV)

Spiritual Tactics, Gear & Weapons	Life Application
Perspective	The real Enemy is not the people we see, but rather Satan and his invisible evil forces. This truth reminds us to rise above offenses and not react. We can set our mind on eternal matters and remain focused on Christ. This way Satan will not be able to play mind games and steal our peace and joy. The proper perspective will allow us to focus on the victory that has already been won at the cross and resurrection.
Preparation	Spiritual preparation is an essential part of the Christian life. With steadfast determination, we can prepare by putting on the full armor of God before and during an attack. We can rely on the Holy Spirit's power to stand our ground. It is wise to pray daily for God's protection for our mind, body, and emotions.
Fasting	Fasting is a powerful way to humble ourselves and seek the Lord's face for wisdom. God is faithful to guide us when we come to Him for direction. During our time of fasting and prayer, we can thank God for His faithfulness in the past and His character that never changes. It is a powerful weapon to pray back God's promises to remind us of God's love. This time of fasting allows us to hear the Lord's whispers when we seek Him for wisdom and direction.
Standing Firm	We recognize that we are powerless in our own strength, but the Lord is all powerful and He promises to fight our battles. God repeatedly tells us to not be afraid or discouraged. The battle is the Lord's, and we can be confident that He will bring about a miraculous outcome. When we stand firm as a Christian community, we are stronger together than apart. There is strength in solidarity. Our job is to show up to the battle, put on our armor of God, and stand firm in our faith.

Worship	We worship a miracle-working God, and He delights in overturning the plans of the Enemy. Just as Jehoshaphat praised the Lord in advance of the battle, so can we. It is a powerful spiritual weapon to praise and thank the Lord. The battle is the Lord's, and He will fight on our behalf while we worship Him. Worship will strengthen our spiritual resolve to trust in the only One who can save us.
Gratitude	Jehoshaphat and his people immediately went to the temple and praised God with grateful hearts for the victorious outcome. The Lord blessed them with peace on every side. When we experience victory over our present-day battles, it is important to immediately thank God for His faithfulness and mercy. Our gratitude is a sweet fragrance to our heavenly Father. Gratitude produces joy for the journey.
Belt of Truth	The belt of truth is one of the most powerful weapons against the master deceiver. When Satan lies to us, we can respond by reciting what is true based on Scripture. Even Jesus did this when He was tempted in the wilderness. God's Word reminds us what is true when accusations rail against us.
Breastplate of Righteousness	When Satan attacks our heart, emotions, and self-worth, we can speak out loud that we stand in the righteousness of Christ and not our own. Christ's breastplate will protect our hearts from the attack and remind us we are worthy and loved because of what Jesus did for us on the cross. He has taken our sin and given us His righteousness in its place. We are the children of God, and we have been cleansed of all our unrighteousness and made right with God.
Shoes of Peace	During a season of turmoil and confusion, we can stand firm and put on the shoes of peace. If we remain focused on Jesus, we will not sink down into the waves of chaos. The Lord has given us His peace to live in harmony with each other and to rise above relational conflict. As believers, the peace of Christ that rules our hearts allows us to be salt and light to a broken world. Keep trusting the Lord and sharing your testimony with others.

Shield of Faith	When Satan shoots his arrows filled with temptation, doubt, and fear, we can put up our shield of faith for protection. The Lord Almighty will cover us with a hedge of protection so we can keep fighting the good fight of faith and press on with perseverance. Our shield of faith protects us against attacks of fear, anxiety, and despair.
Helmet of Salvation	We are prepared for battle when Satan questions our salvation, baptism, or relationship with Jesus. Putting on the helmet of salvation allows us to proclaim with godly confidence that we are saved by the blood of Jesus. Our salvation is secure because of Christ, and our names are written in the Lamb's Book of Life. We have been given God's blessed assurance of our salvation, and that cannot be taken from us. We are sealed by the Holy Spirit.
Sword of the Spirit	The Word of God cuts through every lie, but it also brings clarity, conviction, and healing. God's Word is living water to our souls because it shows us God's heart, character, and His glorious promises. The more we meditate and memorize the Word of God, the better equipped we will be to wield our sword. We can fight on the offensive with the sword of God's Word instead of struggling under condemnation. The sword of God's Word reminds us to focus on what is true, noble, right, pure, and lovely. (Philippians 4:8)
Prayer	It is important to humble ourselves, repent from our sins, and thank God for His faithfulness before we ask for anything. It is important to come to the Lord in prayer with believing faith, not halfhearted unbelief. We need to be spiritually alert and continuously praying for all ambassadors of Christ. Through intercessory prayer, the Lord will give us His wisdom, discernment, and protection right when we need it most. Remember, there is power and divine intervention when we cry out in Jesus's name!

APPENDIX 3
DISCOVERING YOUR KINGDOM
PURPOSE AND DREAMS

*I pray that your hearts will be flooded with light so that you
can understand the confident hope he has given to those he has
called—his holy people who are his rich and glorious inheritance.*

Ephesians 1:18 NLT

C. S. Lewis declared, "You are never too old to set another goal or dream a new dream."[1] The value of a vision, goal, or dream is not dependent on one's age, but rather derived from our Savior—who is our source of inspiration. There are different chapters in the book of life, and I believe you are about to turn the page to begin a brand-new chapter. I wonder what this new chapter will hold for you and your walk with Christ? If you ask me, I believe the best is yet to come. Ask the Lord to plant a dream in your heart that is much bigger than yourself; a dream that will bring God glory. God is faithful, and He never wastes any of our experiences or tears. The Enemy may have attempted to derail your calling, "But the plans of the Lord stand firm forever, the purposes of his heart through all generations" (Psalm 33:11 NIV). Jesus is the author and finisher of our faith, and He always has the final word.

We are all called to know Christ and make Him known. We can be a light for Christ by demonstrating compassion, kindness, and mercy to broken people. "As you love people, serve people, point people towards faith in Christ, redirect wayward people, restore broken people, and develop people into the peak of their spiritual potential, you reaffirm your understanding of your primary mission in the world."[2] If we love God, we will desire to demonstrate His love to others.

Before you dive into the questions below, humbly come to our heavenly Father in prayer and ask for his wisdom to discern God's direction. "Commit to the Lord whatever you do, and He will establish your plans" (Proverbs 16:3 NIV). As you prepare your heart . . . pray fervently, seek earnestly, and spend time 'holy listening' while reflecting on the following questions:

1. Do you have a clear sense of calling on your life? If you are in transition, ask the Lord to reveal His plans and purposes for you.
2. When do you experience the joy of God's presence? During worship? Writing? Being out in nature? Reading Scripture? While praying? Serving in Christian community? Other?
3. List the hardships that God has helped you overcome, navigate, or wrestle through by God's grace. Do you desire to help someone else through similar circumstances?
4. What topics are you passionate about and why?
5. What are the tasks and responsibilities that are life-giving to you, the ones you seem to have endless energy and enthusiasm to accomplish?
6. What are the tasks and responsibilities that are most life-taking and draining to you?
7. What age group do you enjoy working with the most and the least? Explain why.
8. Have you ever had a dream that you put on hold? What was it? Ask God to give you His wisdom to know if it is time to pick it back up or just let it go.
9. After reflecting on all the answers you have written down thus far, what are the common themes rising to the surface?
10. Have you ever taken a spiritual gifts class or filled out a spiritual gifts assessment? What were your top three gifts?
11. Ask your small group and other mature Christ followers which spiritual gifts they see in your life. This should be a confirmation.
12. Meet with a church staff member and ask them how you can use your gifts to build up the church or the local community.
13. Start volunteering in an area of your giftedness.
14. Continue to pray for God's kingdom purpose to be revealed.

———

Trust in the Lord with all your heart
and lean not on your own understanding;
in all your ways submit to him,
and he will make your paths straight.

Proverbs 3:4–5 (NIV)

APPENDIX 4
CTM—CLIMB THE MOUNTAIN
HIKING MINISTRY GUIDE

"God does not want us to simply forget the pain of the past. He wants us to be fruitful in the land of our suffering! Use it for good. Minister to others. Plant seeds of hope."[1] There is a way to embrace our future while acknowledging but not living in the past. More than ever before, people are hungry for hope, and we know the God of all hope. Sharing your cross story is a natural way to discuss how Christ transforms lives. Relational discipleship and conversational evangelism are authentic ways to grow and share your faith. It is not complicated; it is quite simple. Inviting a friend to go for a hike is one way you can reach out to others. You will be amazed how the exercise, sunshine, and fresh air will help to lower your stress as you hike in the beauty of God's creation. After you go for a few hikes, you will quickly see how easy it is to encourage one another through meaningful, discipleship-focused conversations.

You can start your own CTM (Climb the Mountain) Hiking Ministry in your hometown or church. If hiking is too strenuous for your group, you can call it a "walk and talk" ministry. The ministry strategies are easy to adapt to accommodate your group.

- **Outreach:** Invite the people in your Bible study or start with a small group of friends.
- **Purpose:** To create opportunities for relational discipleship and conversational evangelism.
- **Time:** Decide the time and location of the hike and send a reminder text message.
- **Format:** When everyone has arrived at the hiking location, begin by sharing a passage of Scripture or a short devotional, and then pray for your time together. As you hike, you can reflect on the past week and discuss the following discipleship-care questions.

J = Jesus:
How are your faith muscles growing stronger as you place your trust in Christ? Share your personal testimony.

O = Others:
Who did you share the love of Christ with this past week with an act of kindness?

Y = Yourself:
Where do you feel weak and need encouragement or prayer?

- **Planning:** Be sure to get everyone's contact information so you can communicate about future events. Discuss the date and time of the next gathering, whether it is a hike, a social event, or attending a church service together. Remember, there is always room to invite a new friend, and everyone is welcome!

———

Always be prepared to give an answer to everyone who asks you to give the reason for the hope that you have.

1 Peter 3:15 (NIV)

Please post your CTM summit hiking photos on my Instagram or Facebook accounts: @SharonEleanorToddAuthor

ABOUT THE AUTHOR

Sharon Eleanor Todd is a writer who resides in Connecticut and spends her summers in the Adirondack Mountains of New York. She is an artist at heart, adventurer in spirit, and an Adirondack Park enthusiast. Sharon is most content when she is sitting in her favorite Adirondack chair watching the sunrise over the lake with a Bible in one hand and a hot cup of coffee in the other. She is passionate about teaching others how they can grow in their relationship with Christ through one-on-one discipleship, ministry retreats, and training workshops. She is a contagious encourager who enjoys fostering a renewed sense of hope, significance, and purpose. Sharon's various ministry roles have taken place both globally and locally in hospitals, universities, churches, and on hiking trails. Her educational background includes a Bachelor's degree in Psychology/Sociology, a Master's in Educational Leadership, and a Master of Divinity. Sharon's education and ministry experiences have fueled her passion for helping people grow in their faith and lead in their giftedness. For more information, Sharon's website address is www.SharonEleanorTodd.com

ENDNOTES

Chapter 1

1   Anne Graham Lotz, *Why? Trusting God When You Don't Understand* (2004), quoted in *Barbour's Encyclopedia of Great Christian Quotes* (Uhrichsville, OH: Barbour Publishing, 2016), 451.

2   Bill Bright, *The Joy of Faithful Obedience* (2003), quoted in *Barbour's Encyclopedia of Great Christian Quotes* (Uhrichsville, OH: Barbour Publishing, 2016), 236.

3   Amy Carmichael, *Amy Carmichael, A Very Present Help: Life Messages of Great Christians*, compiled by Judith Couchman, (New York: Vine Books, 1996), 34.

4   Joni Eareckson Tada, Facebook quote repost, March 2021.

Climb the Mountain Scene 2

1   Stormie Omartian, *Just Enough Light for the Step I'm On* (1999), quoted in *Barbour's Encyclopedia of Great Christian Quotes* (Uhrichsville, OH: Barbour Publishing, 2016), 452.

Chapter 2

1   Karen Phillips Goodman, *You're Late Again, Lord!* (2002), quoted in *Barbour's Encyclopedia of Great Christian Quotes* (Uhrichsville, OH: Barbour Publishing, 2016), 434.

2   Andrew Murray, *The Master's Indwelling* (1895), quoted in *Barbour's Encyclopedia of Great Christian Quotes* (Uhrichsville, OH: Barbour Publishing, 2016), 434.

3   Henry Cloud and John Townsend, *God Will Make a Way* (2002), quoted in *Barbour's Encyclopedia of Great Christian Quotes* (Uhrichsville, OH: Barbour Publishing, 2016), 453.

4   Amy Carmichael, *A Very Present Help: Life Messages of Great Christians* compiled by Judith Couchman (New York: Vine Books, 1996).

5   Roy Lessin, *Today is Your Best Day* (2006), quoted in *Barbour's Encyclopedia of Great Christian Quotes* (Uhrichsville, OH: Barbour Publishing, 2016), 374.

6   Bruce Wilkinson, *Beyond Jabez* (2005), quoted in *Barbour's Encyclopedia of Great Christian Quotes* (Uhrichsville, OH: Barbour Publishing, 2016), 347.

7   Joseph Stowell, *Through the Fire* (1985), quoted in *Barbour's Encyclopedia of Great Christian Quotes* (Uhrichsville, OH: Barbour Publishing, 2016), 431.

8   John Ortberg, *If You Want to Walk on Water, You've Got to Get Out of the Boat* (2001), quoted in *Barbour's Encyclopedia of Great Christian Quotes* (Uhrichsville, OH: Barbour Publishing, 2016), 146.

9   Steve Campbell, Why More Aren't Healed Sermon (2009), quoted in *Barbour's Encyclopedia of Great Christian Quotes* (Uhrichsville, OH: Barbour Publishing, 2016), 457.

10   John MacArthur, *The MacArthur New Testament Commentary: 1 Corinthians* (1984), quoted in *Barbour's Encyclopedia of Great Christian Quotes* (Uhrichsville, OH: Barbour Publishing, 2016), 390.

11   "Carry Your Cross," contributed by Anitha Jabastion on Aug 4, 2020. https://www.sermoncentral.com/sermon-illustrations/100749/following-jesus-by-anitha-jabastion.

Chapter 3

1   Beth Moore, *Voices of the Faithful* (2005), quoted in *Barbour's Encyclopedia of Great Christian Quotes* (Uhrichsville, OH: Barbour Publishing, 2016), 104.

2   John Calvin, *Bible Commentaries* (16th Century), quoted in *Barbour's Encyclopedia of Great Christian Quotes* (Uhrichsville, OH: Barbour Publishing, 2016), 102.

3   D. L. Moody, *Best Thoughts and Discourses of D. L. Moody* (1876), quoted in *Barbour's Encyclopedia of Great Christian Quotes* (Uhrichsville, OH: Barbour Publishing, 2016), 104.

4   David Jeremiah, *Spiritual Warfare* (1995), quoted in *Barbour's Encyclopedia of Great Christian Quotes* (Uhrichsville, OH: Barbour Publishing, 2016), 102.

5   Shelly Beach, *The Silent Seduction of Self-Talk* (2009), quoted in *Barbour's Encyclopedia of Great Christian Quotes* (Uhrichsville, OH: Barbour Publishing, 2016), 104.

6   Charles Stanley, *When the Enemy Strikes* (2004), quoted in *Barbour's Encyclopedia of Great Christian Quotes* (Uhrichsville, OH: Barbour Publishing, 2016), 102.

7   Corrie ten Boom, *Amazing Love* (1953), quoted in *Barbour's Encyclopedia of Great Christian Quotes* (Uhrichsville, OH: Barbour Publishing, 2016), 103.

8   Tony Evans, *Tony Evans Speaks Out* (2000), quoted in *Barbour's Encyclopedia of Great Christian Quotes* (Uhrichsville, OH: Barbour Publishing, 2016), 103.

9   Adrian Rogers, "Unmasking False Prophets" (2007) quoted in *Barbour's Encyclopedia of Great Christian Quotes* (Uhrichsville, OH: Barbour Publishing, 2016), 102.

10   Billy Graham, *The Journey* (2006), quoted in *Barbour's Encyclopedia of Great Christian Quotes* (Uhrichsville, OH: Barbour Publishing, 2016), 102.

11   Tony Evans, *God Cannot Be Trusted* (And Five Other Lies of Satan) (2005), quoted in *Barbour's Encyclopedia of Great Christian Quotes* (Uhrichsville, OH: Barbour Publishing, 2016), 102.

12   Evans, *God Cannot*, quoted in *Barbour's Encyclopedia of Great Christian Quotes* (Uhrichsville, OH: Barbour Publishing, 2016), 102.

13   John Piper, *God is the Gospel* (2005), quoted in *Barbour's Encyclopedia of Great Christian Quotes* (Uhrichsville, OH: Barbour Publishing, 2016), 102.

14   Beth Moore, *Praying God's Word* (2000), quoted in *Barbour's Encyclopedia of Great Christian Quotes* (Uhrichsville, OH: Barbour Publishing, 2016), 102.

15   Plaque Description about the Bog plant at the Wild Center in Tupper Lake, NY.

16   Plaque Description about the Bog plant at the Wild Center in Tupper Lake, NY.

17   Henry Cloud and John Townsend, *Safe People* (2005), quoted in *Barbour's Encyclopedia of Great Christian Quotes* (Uhrichsville, OH: Barbour Publishing, 2016), 81.

18   L. B. Cowman, *Streams in the Desert: 366 Daily Devotional Readings*, edited by Jim Reimann (Grand Rapids: Zondervan, 1997), 60.

19   Kay Arthur, *When Bad Things Happen* (2002), quoted in *Barbour's Encyclopedia of Great Christian Quotes* (Uhrichsville, OH: Barbour Publishing, 2016), 439.

20   Elizabeth George, *A Woman after God's Own Heart* (1997), quoted in *Barbour's Encyclopedia of Great Christian Quotes* (Uhrichsville, OH: Barbour Publishing, 2016), 352.

21   Mary Southerland, *Experiencing God's Power in Your Ministry* (2006), quoted in *Barbour's Encyclopedia of Great Christian Quotes* (Uhrichsville, OH: Barbour Publishing, 2016), 147.

22   Brendan O'Rourke and DeEtte Sauer, *Hope of Homecoming* (2003), quoted in *Barbour's Encyclopedia of Great Christian Quotes* (Uhrichsville, OH: Barbour Publishing, 2016), 146.

23   Jay Abramson, Valley Community Baptist Church Sermon, (2010).

24   David Jeremiah, *Spiritual Warfare* (1995), quoted in *Barbour's Encyclopedia of Great Christian Quotes* (Uhrichsville, OH: Barbour Publishing, 2016), 102.

25   Stormie Omartian, *The Power of a Praying Wife* (1997), quoted in *Barbour's Encyclopedia of Great Christian Quotes* (Uhrichsville, OH: Barbour Publishing, 2016), 104.

26   Frances Frangipane, *The Three Battlegrounds* (1989), quoted in *Barbour's Encyclopedia of Great Christian Quotes* (Uhrichsville, OH: Barbour Publishing, 2016), 439.

27   Max Lucado, *A Gentle Thunder* (1995), quoted in *Barbour's Encyclopedia of Great Christian Quotes* (Uhrichsville, OH: Barbour Publishing, 2016), 38.

28   Leslie Haskin, *God Has Not Forgotten About You* (2009), quoted in *Barbour's Encyclopedia of Great Christian Quotes* (Uhrichsville, OH: Barbour Publishing, 2016), 440.

29   Neil T. Anderson, *Victory Over the Darkness: Realize the Power of Your Destiny in Christ* (Ventura, CA: Regal Books, 2000), 162.

30   Warren Wiersbe, *The Strategy of Satan: How to Detect Him and Defeat Him* (Carol Stream, IL: Tyndale House Publishers, 1979), 144.

Chapter 4

1   Marlene Bagnull, *Write His Answer* (1990), quoted in *Barbour's Encyclopedia of Great Christian Quotes* (Uhrichsville, OH: Barbour Publishing, 2016), 462.

2   Martin Luther, *Table Talk* (16th Century), quoted in *Barbour's Encyclopedia of Great Christian Quotes* (Uhrichsville, OH: Barbour Publishing, 2016), 476.

3   Hank Hanegraaff, *The Covering* (2002), quoted in *Barbour's Encyclopedia of Great Christian Quotes* (Uhrichsville, OH: Barbour Publishing, 2016), 462.

4   Bill McCartney, *Blind Spots* (2003), quoted in *Barbour's Encyclopedia of Great Christian Quotes* (Uhrichsville, OH: Barbour Publishing, 2016), 463.

5   Kay Arthur, *Speak to My Heart, God* (1993), quoted in *Barbour's Encyclopedia of Great Christian Quotes* (Uhrichsville, OH: Barbour Publishing, 2016), 463.

6   Corrie ten Boom, *Amazing Love* (1953), quoted in *Barbour's Encyclopedia of Great Christian Quotes* (Uhrichsville, OH: Barbour Publishing, 2016), 476.

7   Oswald Chambers, *Approved Unto God* (1941), quoted in *Barbour's Encyclopedia of Great Christian Quotes* (Uhrichsville, OH: Barbour Publishing, 2016), 477.

8   Andy Stanley, *Louder Than Words* (2004), quoted in *Barbour's Encyclopedia of Great Christian Quotes* (Uhrichsville, OH: Barbour Publishing, 2016), 463.

9   Bill Hybels, *Too Busy Not to Pray* (1988), quoted in *Barbour's Encyclopedia of Great Christian Quotes* (Uhrichsville, OH: Barbour Publishing, 2016), 353.

10   John Muir, *My First Summer in the Sierras* (Mineola, NY: Dover Publications, 2004).

11   Sadhu Sundar Singh, *At the Master's Feet* (20th Century), quoted in *Barbour's Encyclopedia of Great Christian Quotes* (Uhrichsville, OH: Barbour Publishing, 2016), 463.

12   Grace Ketterman and Kathy King, *Caring for Your Elderly Parent* (2001), quoted in *Barbour's Encyclopedia of Great Christian Quotes* (Uhrichsville, OH: Barbour Publishing, 2016), 152.

13   David Jeremiah, *Spiritual Warfare* (1995), quoted in *Barbour's Encyclopedia of Great Christian Quotes* (Uhrichsville, OH: Barbour Publishing, 2016), 463.

14   Warren Wiersbe, *Be What You Are* (1988), quoted in *Barbour's Encyclopedia of Great Christian Quotes* (Uhrichsville, OH: Barbour Publishing, 2016), 471.

Climb the Mountain Scene 5

1   Merriam-Webster, "erratic," https://www.merriam-webster.com/dictionary/erratic.

Chapter 5

1   Rick Warren, *The Purpose Driven Life* (2002), quoted in *Barbour's Encyclopedia of Great Christian Quotes* (Uhrichsville, OH: Barbour Publishing, 2016), 339.

2   Suzanne Lance. Heaven Up-h'isted-ness . . . The History of the Adirondack Forty Sixers and the High Peaks of the Adirondacks (2011), Adirondack Forty-Sixers, Inc.

3   George Fox, personal Letter (17th Century), quoted in *Barbour's Encyclopedia of Great Christian Quotes* (Uhrichsville, OH: Barbour Publishing, 2016), 439.

4   Beth Moore, "Who Do You Trust?" teaching series (2007), quoted in *Barbour's Encyclopedia of Great Christian Quotes* (Uhrichsville, OH: Barbour Publishing, 2016), 96.

5   Everett Worthington, *Forgiving and Reconciling* (2003), quoted in *Barbour's Encyclopedia of Great Christian Quotes* (Uhrichsville, OH: Barbour Publishing, 2016), 152.

6   Greg Laurie, *Wrestling with God* (2003), quoted in *Barbour's Encyclopedia of Great Christian Quotes* (Uhrichsville, OH: Barbour Publishing, 2016), 151.

7   Charles Swindoll, *Improving Your Serve* (1981), quoted in *Barbour's Encyclopedia of Great Christian Quotes* (Uhrichsville, OH: Barbour Publishing, 2016), 151.

8   Corrie ten Boom, *He Cares, He Comforts* (1997), quoted in *Barbour's Encyclopedia of Great Christian Quotes* (Uhrichsville, OH: Barbour Publishing, 2016), 151.

9   Bruce Wilkinson, *The Dream Giver* (2003), quoted in *Barbour's Encyclopedia of Great Christian Quotes* (Uhrichsville, OH: Barbour Publishing, 2016), 146.

10   Anne Graham Lotz, *The Daily Light Journal* (2004), quoted in *Barbour's Encyclopedia of Great Christian Quotes* (Uhrichsville, OH: Barbour Publishing, 2016), 96.

11   Virginia Ann Froehle, *Loving Yourself More* (1993), quoted in *Barbour's Encyclopedia of Great Christian Quotes* (Uhrichsville, OH: Barbour Publishing, 2016), 336.

12   Ravi Zacharias, *Beyond Opinion* (2007), quoted in *Barbour's Encyclopedia of Great Christian Quotes* (Uhrichsville, OH: Barbour Publishing, 2016), 235.

13   Max Lucado, *Come Thirsty* (2004), quoted in *Barbour's Encyclopedia of Great Christian Quotes* (Uhrichsville, OH: Barbour Publishing, 2016), 336.

14   Hank Hanegraaff, *The Covering* (2002), quoted in *Barbour's Encyclopedia of Great Christian Quotes* (Uhrichsville, OH: Barbour Publishing, 2016), 336.

15   Bertha Spafford Vester, *Our Jerusalem: An American Family in the Holy City, 1881–1949* (Chicago: Ariel Publishing House, 1988).

16   Michael Card, *Scribbling in the Sand* (2002), quoted in *Barbour's Encyclopedia of Great Christian Quotes* (Uhrichsville, OH: Barbour Publishing, 2016), 86.

17   D. L. Moody, "The Transfiguration" Sermon (19th Century), quoted in *Barbour's Encyclopedia of Great Christian Quotes* (Uhrichsville, OH: Barbour Publishing, 2016), 436.

18   Bruce Wilkinson, *Beyond Jabez* (2005), quoted in *Barbour's Encyclopedia of Great Christian Quotes* (Uhrichsville, OH: Barbour Publishing, 2016), 436.

19   Charles Stanley, *Winning the War Within* (1998), quoted in *Barbour's Encyclopedia of Great Christian Quotes* (Uhrichsville, OH: Barbour Publishing, 2016), 437.

20   Charles Spurgeon, "Consecration to God" sermon (1868), quoted in *Barbour's Encyclopedia of Great Christian Quotes* (Uhrichsville, OH: Barbour Publishing, 2016), 398.

Chapter 6

1   Beth Moore, *Breaking Free* (1999), quoted in *Barbour's Encyclopedia of Great Christian Quotes* (Uhrichsville, OH: Barbour Publishing, 2016), 42.

2   Hannah Whitall Smith, *The God of All Comfort* (1906), quoted in *Barbour's Encyclopedia of Great Christian Quotes* (Uhrichsville, OH: Barbour Publishing, 2016), 204.

3   Greg Laurie, *The Upside Down Church* (1999), quoted in *Barbour's Encyclopedia of Great Christian Quotes* (Uhrichsville, OH: Barbour Publishing, 2016), 271.

4   Jerry Bridges, *The Practice of Godliness* (1996), quoted in *Barbour's Encyclopedia of Great Christian Quotes* (Uhrichsville, OH: Barbour Publishing, 2016), 204.

5   Charles Stanley, *30 Life Principles Study Guide* (2008), quoted in *Barbour's Encyclopedia of Great Christian Quotes* (Uhrichsville, OH: Barbour Publishing, 2016), 42.

6   Bill Gillham, *Lifetime Guarantee* (1993), quoted in *Barbour's Encyclopedia of Great Christian Quotes* (Uhrichsville, OH: Barbour Publishing, 2016), 204.

7   Joseph Stowell, *Tongue in Check* (1983), quoted in *Barbour's Encyclopedia of Great Christian Quotes* (Uhrichsville, OH: Barbour Publishing, 2016), 229.

8   Franklin Graham, *All for Jesus* (2003), quoted in *Barbour's Encyclopedia of Great Christian Quotes* (Uhrichsville, OH: Barbour Publishing, 2016), 229.

9   Watchman Nee, *The Release of the Spirit* (1965), quoted in *Barbour's Encyclopedia of Great Christian Quotes* (Uhrichsville, OH: Barbour Publishing, 2016), 42.

10   Jane Rubietta, *Between Two Gardens* (2001), quoted in *Barbour's Encyclopedia of Great Christian Quotes* (Uhrichsville, OH: Barbour Publishing, 2016), 28.

11   Beth Moore, "Wrestling with God" teaching series (2009), quoted in *Barbour's Encyclopedia of Great Christian Quotes* (Uhrichsville, OH: Barbour Publishing, 2016), 340.

12   Bruce Carroll, *Sometimes Miracles Hide* (1999), quoted in *Barbour's Encyclopedia of Great Christian Quotes* (Uhrichsville, OH: Barbour Publishing, 2016), 365.

13   James MacDonald, *Lord, Change My Attitude* (2001), quoted in *Barbour's Encyclopedia of Great Christian Quotes* (Uhrichsville, OH: Barbour Publishing, 2016), 114.

14   Joel Osteen, *Your Best Life Now* (2004), quoted in *Barbour's Encyclopedia of Great Christian Quotes* (Uhrichsville, OH: Barbour Publishing, 2016), 365.

15   Susan Vaughn. *Half Empty, Half Full* (2000), quoted in *Barbour's Encyclopedia of Great Christian Quotes* (Uhrichsville, OH: Barbour Publishing, 2016), 225.

16   Jentezen Franklin, *Believe That You Can* (2008), quoted in *Barbour's Encyclopedia of Great Christian Quotes* (Uhrichsville, OH: Barbour Publishing, 2016), 225.

17   Jackson Crum, sermon quote from the Israel trip with Park Community Church, Chicago, IL (2005).

18   Anne Lamott, *Traveling Mercies* (1999), quoted in *Barbour's Encyclopedia of Great Christian Quotes* (Uhrichsville, OH: Barbour Publishing, 2016), 82.

19   Carol Kent, *A New Kind of Normal* (2007), quoted in *Barbour's Encyclopedia of Great Christian Quotes* (Uhrichsville, OH: Barbour Publishing, 2016), 82.

20   Roy Lessin, *Today Is Your Best Day* (2006), quoted in *Barbour's Encyclopedia of Great Christian Quotes* (Uhrichsville, OH: Barbour Publishing, 2016), 261.

21   Kay Arthur, *When Bad Things Happen* (2002), quoted in *Barbour's Encyclopedia of Great Christian Quotes* (Uhrichsville, OH: Barbour Publishing, 2016), 313.

22   Hannah Whithall Smith, *The God of All Comfort* (1906), quoted in *Barbour's Encyclopedia of Great Christian Quotes* (Uhrichsville, OH: Barbour Publishing, 2016), 204.

23   Kay Arthur, *When Bad Things Happen* (2002), quoted in *Barbour's Encyclopedia of Great Christian Quotes* (Uhrichsville, OH: Barbour Publishing, 2016), 259.

24   Timothy Keller, *The Reason for God* (2008), quoted in *Barbour's Encyclopedia of Great Christian Quotes* (Uhrichsville, OH: Barbour Publishing, 2016), 225.

25   Max Lucado, *In the Eye of the Storm* (1991), quoted in *Barbour's Encyclopedia of Great Christian Quotes* (Uhrichsville, OH: Barbour Publishing, 2016), 430.

26   Warren Wiersbe, *Be What You Are* (1988), quoted in *Barbour's Encyclopedia of Great Christian Quotes* (Uhrichsville, OH: Barbour Publishing, 2016), 433.

27   Sharon Jaynes, *Your Scars are Beautiful to God* (2006), quoted in *Barbour's Encyclopedia of Great Christian Quotes* (Uhrichsville, OH: Barbour Publishing, 2016), 312.

Climb the Mountain Scene 7

1   Jim Cymbala, *You Were Made for More* (2008), quoted in *Barbour's Encyclopedia of Great Christian Quotes* (Uhrichsville, OH: Barbour Publishing, 2016), 434.

2   Oswald Chambers, *Approved Unto God* (20th Century), quoted in *Barbour's Encyclopedia of Great Christian Quotes* (Uhrichsville, OH: Barbour Publishing, 2016), 196.

Chapter 7

1 Dallas Willard, *The Spirit of the Disciplines* (1988), quoted in *Barbour's Encyclopedia of Great Christian Quotes* (Uhrichsville, OH: Barbour Publishing, 2016), 109.

2 Jim Cymbala and Stephen Sorenson, *The Church God Blesses* (2002), quoted in *Barbour's Encyclopedia of Great Christian Quotes* (Uhrichsville, OH: Barbour Publishing, 2016), 44.

3 John Ortberg, *God Is Closer than You Think* (2005), quoted in *Barbour's Encyclopedia of Great Christian Quotes* (Uhrichsville, OH: Barbour Publishing, 2016), 310.

4 Bill Bright and John Damoose. *Red Sky in the Morning* (1998), quoted in *Barbour's Encyclopedia of Great Christian Quotes* (Uhrichsville, OH: Barbour Publishing, 2016), 44.

5 Matthew Henry, *Commentary on the Whole Bible* (1706), quoted in *Barbour's Encyclopedia of Great Christian Quotes* (Uhrichsville, OH: Barbour Publishing, 2016), 214.

6 Charles Spurgeon, "God in the Covenant" sermon (1856), quoted in *Barbour's Encyclopedia of Great Christian Quotes* (Uhrichsville, OH: Barbour Publishing, 2016), 213.

7 Kirk Cameron and Ray Comfort, *Life's Emergency Handbook* (2002), quoted in *Barbour's Encyclopedia of Great Christian Quotes* (Uhrichsville, OH: Barbour Publishing, 2016), 215.

8 Philip Yancey, *Prayer: Does It Make Any Difference?* (2006), quoted in *Barbour's Encyclopedia of Great Christian Quotes* (Uhrichsville, OH: Barbour Publishing, 2016), 461.

9 Peter Taylor Forsyth, *The Work of Christ* (1909), quoted in *Barbour's Encyclopedia of Great Christian Quotes* (Uhrichsville, OH: Barbour Publishing, 2016), 374.

10 Mark Buchanan, *The Rest of God* (2006), quoted in *Barbour's Encyclopedia of Great Christian Quotes* (Uhrichsville, OH: Barbour Publishing, 2016), 156.

11 Randy Alcorn, *The Grace and Truth Paradox* (2003), quoted in *Barbour's Encyclopedia of Great Christian Quotes* (Uhrichsville, OH: Barbour Publishing, 2016), 374.

12 Erwin Lutzer, *After You've Blown It* (2004), quoted in *Barbour's Encyclopedia of Great Christian Quotes* (Uhrichsville, OH: Barbour Publishing, 2016), 374.

13 Charles Swindoll, "Visiting the Real Twilight Zone" sermon series (1985), quoted in *Barbour's Encyclopedia of Great Christian Quotes* (Uhrichsville, OH: Barbour Publishing, 2016), 122.

14 Joel Rosenberg, *Epicenter* (2003), quoted in *Barbour's Encyclopedia of Great Christian Quotes* (Uhrichsville, OH: Barbour Publishing, 2016), 22.

15 Andy Stanley, *The Principle of the Path* (2008), quoted in *Barbour's Encyclopedia of Great Christian Quotes* (Uhrichsville, OH: Barbour Publishing, 2016), 95.

16   Karol Ladd, *The Power of a Positive Woman* (2002), quoted in *Barbour's Encyclopedia of Great Christian Quotes* (Uhrichsville, OH: Barbour Publishing, 2016),256.

17   Chuck Swindoll, *Laugh Again* (1995), quoted in *Barbour's Encyclopedia of Great Christian Quotes* (Uhrichsville, OH: Barbour Publishing, 2016), 256.

18   Martyn Lloyd-Jones, *Love So Amazing* (1962), quoted in *Barbour's Encyclopedia of Great Christian Quotes* (Uhrichsville, OH: Barbour Publishing, 2016), 440.

19   Wendy Widder, *Living Whole* (2000), quoted in *Barbour's Encyclopedia of Great Christian Quotes* (Uhrichsville, OH: Barbour Publishing, 2016), 256.

20   Max Lucado, *Come Thirsty* (2003), quoted in *Barbour's Encyclopedia of Great Christian Quotes* (Uhrichsville, OH: Barbour Publishing, 2016), 282.

21   L. B. Cowman, *Streams in the Desert*. Zondervan Publishing. Grand Rapids, MI, 1997, p.418.

22   Brendan O'Rourke and DeEtte Sauer, *Hope of Homecoming* (2003), quoted in *Barbour's Encyclopedia of Great Christian Quotes* (Uhrichsville, OH: Barbour Publishing, 2016), 212.

23   Lloyd John Olivia, *The Magnificent Vision* (1980), quoted in *Barbour's Encyclopedia of Great Christian Quotes* (Uhrichsville, OH: Barbour Publishing, 2016), 256.

24   Chuck Swindoll, *Laugh Again* (1995), quoted in *Barbour's Encyclopedia of Great Christian Quotes* (Uhrichsville, OH: Barbour Publishing, 2016), 256.

25   Michael Youssef, "Joy Though Christ" (2010), quoted in *Barbour's Encyclopedia of Great Christian Quotes* (Uhrichsville, OH: Barbour Publishing, 2016), 256.

26   Joe Beam, *Getting Past Guilt* (2003). quoted in *Barbour's Encyclopedia of Great Christian Quotes* (Uhrichsville, OH: Barbour Publishing, 2016), 257.

27   Bob Moorehead, *A Passion for Victory* (1996), quoted in *Barbour's Encyclopedia of Great Christian Quotes* (Uhrichsville, OH: Barbour Publishing, 2016), 461.

28   Jill Briscoe, *The New Normal* (2005), quoted in *Barbour's Encyclopedia of Great Christian Quotes* (Uhrichsville, OH: Barbour Publishing, 2016), 466.

Appendix 3

1   C. S. Lewis, quoted in 16 Amazing Christian Quotes about Imagination and Dreams, www.Christian quotes.info. December 1. 2019 by Pastor Jack Wellman.

2   Bill Hybels, *Walk Across the Room* (2006), quoted in *Barbour's Encyclopedia of Great Christian Quotes* (Uhrichsville, OH: Barbour Publishing, 2016), 204.

Appendix 4

1   Sharon Jaynes, *Your Scars Are Beautiful to God* (2006), quoted in *Barbour's Encyclopedia of Great Christian Quotes* (Uhrichsville, OH: Barbour Publishing, 2016), 312.

ORDER INFORMATION

REDEMPTION
P R E S S

To order additional copies of this book, please visit
www.redemption-press.com.
Also available at Amazon, Christian bookstores,
and Barnes and Noble.

CPSIA information can be obtained
at www.ICGtesting.com
Printed in the USA
JSHW020631110822
29159JS00004B/14